The
Power
of Hope

365 DAILY DEVOTIONS

BroadStreet Publishing Group, LLC.
Savage, Minnesota, USA
Broadstreetpublishing.com

The Power of Hope

© 2024 by BroadStreet Publishing®

9781424567966
9781424567973 (eBook)

Devotional entries composed by Sara Perry.

Typesetting and design by Garborg Design Works | garborgdesign.com

Editorial services by Michelle Winger | literallyprecise.com, Carole Holdahl, and Raya Forsberg

Printed in China.

24 25 26 27 28 29 30   7 6 5 4 3 2 1

Let all that I am
wait quietly before God,
for my hope is in him.
He alone is my rock
and my salvation,
my fortress where
I will not be shaken.

PSALM 62:5-6 NLT

Introduction

Hope is a powerful weapon against feelings of helplessness, stress, and dissatisfaction. It increases happiness and improves our quality of life by helping us to remain committed to goals and by motivating us to act. Hope gives us a reason to keep fighting through the tough days, believing that our circumstances will improve.

Where we place our hope is critical. If we hope for temporary things, whether we achieve them or not, we are left wanting. But when we hope in what is eternal, our longing is quenched in the stream of God's love. His presence assures us that we are never alone. The sacrifice Jesus made secured our redemption and reconciled us to our very good Father. Our future is certain. Our present circumstances can be endured. We can thrive, knowing that our inheritance is to spend eternity with our amazing Creator.

Be encouraged and strengthened as you read these Scriptures, devotions, and applications that give practical wisdom for engaging in the power of hope.

January

"For I know the plans I have for you," declares the Lord, "plans to prosper you and not to harm you, plans to give you hope and a future."

JEREMIAH 29:11 NIV

Active Hope

"Is not your fear of God your confidence,
and the integrity of your ways your hope?"

JOB 4:6 ESV

Chances are hope is much more than you imagine it to be. It is not the same as wishful thinking. It involves both optimism and a plan toward a goal. It is specific and active. If you thought hope was the same as optimism, you are not alone. However, the science behind hope reveals that it is much more than that. It helps us set and reach our goals.

When we are motivated by hope, we are able to set a plan in motion to reach it. True hope does not cause us to sit back and accept that our lives are constant and immovable. It propels us and hands us the keys of ownership to move ahead with integrity. It keeps our hearts rooted in confidence in the one who holds all things together. Today, if all you do is reevaluate your understanding of hope, it is a step toward living with more intention.

Think through your life and the areas where hope has moved you ahead toward a goal. What areas of your life need hope today?

Getting Unstuck

Let us run with endurance the race that lies before us,
keeping our eyes on Jesus,
the pioneer and perfecter of our faith.

HEBREWS 12:1-2 NASB

The ways of Christ help us move out of old ways into new rhythms of living. The power of Christ's message, life, and miracles cannot be overstated. He is the way, the truth, and the life. If we need a fresh burst of living hope, looking to Christ is an answer that will not disappoint.

Hope challenges us to grow in new ways, putting into practice new ideas and following new ways of doing things. Jesus challenged both the powerful and the humble of his day by inviting them to do just that. He offered a different perspective of God the Father. When we feel bogged down by the world and the failure of doing things as we have for too long, Christ offers us the wisdom of hope to reorient and direct us on new paths that lead to life. Let's fix our eyes on him and follow in his footsteps!

Today, read through some of the Sermon on the Mount (found in Matthew 5-7) and put into practice one of Jesus' teachings.

Building Blocks

Encourage each other and build each other up,
just as you are already doing.

1 THESSALONIANS 5:11 NLT

A culture of support is incredibly important within our faith communities. When we know that we can depend on others for encouragement and help when we need it, hope will spring from the soil of our interdependence. God created us for community, one that is lifegiving, transformative, and encouraging. In communities that support and uplift each member, it has been shown that an atmosphere of hope is cultivated.

If you want a practical way to build hope in your own life, or in the lives of those around you, take seriously the advice of Paul in today's verse. He doesn't mean that you should say things that are disingenuous. Encouragement can be anything from reassurance to gratitude. It can be as simple as calling attention to a strength you see in someone in the face of a struggle. Whatever form your encouragement takes, be intentional about it.

Look for genuine ways to encourage those in your life today, from coworkers to family to friends. Pay attention to how you feel afterward.

New Beginnings

"There is hope for a tree,
When it is cut down, that it will sprout again,
And its shoots will not fail."

JOB 14:7 NASB

We are never without hope. Not even when our lives are torn apart, or we experience devastating losses. Today's verse reminds us that even when a tree is cut down, there is hope that it will sprout again. If a torn-down tree can grow new life, so can our lives, even when they are cut down to the stump.

The seeds of life only need the right conditions to grow. Consider how precious jewels are created in the dark under pressure. Pearls are formed violently within clamshells from friction and sand. We may just find that the most beautiful treasures of our lives are formed and revealed in our greatest troubles too. Hope keeps us going and leads us on. If we are living, there is hope for a new start and redemption. We are never too far gone from the restorative power of God—no, never!

Hearing the stories of others who have risen from the ashes of their own lives can encourage you in your time of defeat. Take time to listen or read someone else's story of hope and let it encourage your heart in regard to your own story.

Stronger Together

Let us consider how we may spur one another on toward love and good deeds, not giving up meeting together, as some are in the habit of doing, but encouraging one another—and all the more as you see the Day approaching.

HEBREWS 10:24-25 NIV

In the company of others, we find encouragement to persevere through hard times. We can support one another when we don't have it in us to support ourselves. In short, we need each other. Reliance and need are intrinsically human, we were not created to go through life on our own. When we feel isolated from others, whether through our experiences or by physical distance, we may find it harder to hold onto hope.

Hope is a resource for coping during hard times. When we are connected to communities with whom we can share our experiences in a real way, we may find that the significance of being seen and met is enough to propel us in hope. Instead of trying to get by or get out of a funk on our own, the power of being met as we become transparent with others is found in the beauty of connection. It can be the difference between just barely surviving and reorienting in hope toward a better future.

Today, whether in person, or in some other way, talk intentionally about what is going on in your life with someone you trust.

Invigorating Life Within

To them God willed to make known what are the
riches of the glory of this mystery among the Gentiles:
which is Christ in you, the hope of glory.

COLOSSIANS 1:27 NKJV

When we focus on the good that is already present within
our lives, we can more readily grow in hope as we look with
peace and confidence toward the future. Though we long for
Christ to return, we have the Spirit of God alive within us. He is
always accessible as he works in love and power. The hope of
glory is present in us.

We are not our own and in the best ways. We are not left
alone to our own destructive ways when we submit ourselves
to Christ. We have the living power of his love to transform us.
He loves us to life, time and time again; as he does, we get to
walk with him throughout this life. What a glorious hope we
have in him!

*As you make choices throughout your day, consider how
God feels about them. Invite him into your decision making,
no matter how small the choice. Let hope, peace, love, and
courage compel you.*

Strengthened in Hope

We continually recall before God our Father the things you have done because of your faith and the work you have done because of your love. And we thank him that you continue to be strong because of your hope in our Lord Jesus Christ.

1 THESSALONIANS 1:3 NCV

Studies show that hope leads to greater resilience in those who practice it. Resilience is the ability to withstand difficulties as well as recover quickly from them when they do occur. For those who practice hope, they are not simply wishing for better days. They know that they must weather the hard days along with the good, and it does not break them.

In Christ, everyone is invited to yield to him, even those of us who have lost hope. Hope is much more accessible than we may realize, just as Christ is. As soon as we turn to God, we have our Father's help. The psalms illustrate this over and over again. Even when all seems lost, we can call on God for help. He not only comes to our aid, but he also puts his power behind the small crumbs of our offerings. He turns ashes into beauty, and he won't ever stop doing that!

Read Psalm 56. Bring verse nine to mind every time you need a reminder of God's faithfulness to those who call on him.

Inspired to Do Good

May the Lord Jesus Christ and our Father God, who loved us and in his wonderful grace gave us eternal comfort and a beautiful hope that cannot fail, encourage your hearts and inspire you with strength to always do and speak what is good and beautiful in his eyes.

2 THESSALONIANS 2:16-17 TPT

Hope is not the only end goal; it is also the path that leads us there. Even when our dreams don't seem accessible, we should fix our attention on the necessary steps to move toward them. We don't have to know the exact makeup of our dreams to make significant steps forward. In fact, if we get too caught up in our vision of them, we may become discouraged by the need to adjust our expectations.

Hope inspires us to do what is in front of us. The way we do things is often more important than what we are doing. As long as we are reflecting the values of Christ's kingdom—his love, joy, peace, patience, and kindness—we walk in the light of his nature. Let's take our inspiration from who God is and endeavor to be more like him in our interactions with others.

Pick an attribute of God's character in which you want to grow in more and take steps to be more mindful in practicing and incorporating it into your life today.

Our Standard of Hope

To this end we toil and strive,
because we have our hope set on the living God,
who is the Savior of all people,
especially of those who believe.

1 TIMOTHY 4:10 ESV

If we are not intentional about checking in with the Lord about our mindsets, we can set our hopes and expectations of him too low. The living God does not disappoint. He is always overflowing in mercy and kindness, moving in gracious generosity, and bringing life out of decay. Nothing is impossible with God! He is our standard of hope; he can move mountains, breathe life into dry bones, and heal the sick.

As humans, we struggle with a negativity bias; we often use negative information to deliberate on more than positive. We are prone to remembering the occasional bad thing rather than the consistent good. However, the good news is that this is like a muscle; as you train it, you can strengthen and build your association with what is good, lovely, and true. You can improve your relationship with hope. It will be easier to take steps in the freedom of what is going right rather than focusing on what could go wrong.

For every negative thought you become aware of today, note three positive that are also true. As you do, you will train yourself to look for the good.

The Source

Instruct those who are rich in the present age not to be arrogant or to set their hope on the uncertainty of wealth, but on God, who richly provides us with all things to enjoy.

1 TIMOTHY 6:17 CSB

When we place our hope in things that are bound to change, we set ourselves up for disappointment and discouragement. That is not to say that we can't enjoy these things. Of course, we can! But putting our hope in the shifting systems and our own accounts of things will disappoint. Markets shift and change, and so will our lives. When we put our hope in the unchanging one, the one who created all things and in whom all things find their being, we will not be disappointed.

We cannot accurately predict the way things will be a year from now, let alone ten years from now. We can, however, join our hearts to the one who does. As we stay humble before him, we can weather the storms that life brings with our hope intact. We can learn from what we go through and allow our understanding to expand. God provides all we need, and he shows us the way to truly enjoy life as we join in fellowship with him throughout it.

At the end of the day, evaluate what made you most excited, what stood out to you, and how you responded to difficulties. Consider how your thoughts reveal your expectations. Ask for his help to put your hope in him and to keep it there.

Confidence Builder

Because of his grace he made us right in his sight
and gave us confidence that we will inherit eternal life.

TITUS 3:7 NLT

When we learn to rely on God's grace instead of solely on our own abilities, we allow our hearts to strengthen in confidence. We don't have to second guess ourselves constantly when we walk hand-in-hand with our Good Shepherd. He leads us with peace and his persistent help is there whenever we need it. His grace is always more than enough, and it is a free-flowing fountain that we can drink from no matter how many times we come before him.

God offers us the covering and promise of salvation, not because of anything we have done or could do, but because of his overwhelming faithful love he has toward us. As we join our hearts to him, we can be confident that his goodness is present, and it will continue to be even as we go through the dark valleys of this life. There is nowhere we can go to escape his Spirit or evade his love! What more confidence do we need?

Instead of trying to do things perfectly today, practice grace with yourself and others. Let what is here and now be enough and lean on the faithfulness of God to fill in the cracks.

Reliable Anchor

This hope we have as an anchor of the soul,
a hope both sure and reliable
and one which enters within the veil.

HEBREWS 6:19 NASB

Hope goes deeper than our circumstances and superficial wishes. It is connected to a richer meaning in life. Hope is intrinsically tied to our beliefs. If we believe that God is who he says he is and will faithfully fulfill every promise he has made, our hope is in him. If we believe that we are only as good as our mood is in any given moment, our hope is less like an anchor and more like a kite that can only soar under specific conditions. When we align our hearts and minds with Christ, we throw the anchor of our hope into the ocean of his love. Regardless of our circumstances, that hope remains strong and true.

We may think of our beliefs as static, but hope is quite active. Our beliefs inform our decisions, which in turn inform our actions. We can grow our hope by taking active steps in faith. Perseverance is a part of this, too. Though motivation may move us to put our hope in Christ, persistence and consistency keep us there.

When you start limiting yourself because you fear an outcome, endeavor to choose the faith and thoughts that align with hope.

Living and Active

Praise be to the God and Father of our Lord Jesus Christ! In his great mercy he has given us new birth into a living hope through the resurrection of Jesus Christ from the dead.

1 PETER 1:3 NIV

In Christ's resurrected life, we come alive. Every death and devastation is an opportunity for fresh hope because the source of our hope is alive, and he has not stopped moving in miraculous mercy! His redemptive power is as active today as it has ever been. Instead of giving up in the face of overwhelming odds, we can join our hearts and hope to Christ. He is faithful, reliable, and true.

Even in our grief, we have an insurmountable hope. First Thessalonians 4:13 says, "Do not grieve as those who have no hope." To be clear, it doesn't say not to grieve! It doesn't say to not mourn our losses. No, in fact 2 Corinthians 4:8 reminds us that even in our suffering, we are not without hope: "We are hard pressed on every side, but not crushed; perplexed, but not in despair." No matter what we are facing, we keep going; for there is more ahead than we leave behind.

Write a list of reasons to keep going when you may feel like giving up. Put it in an easily accessible place where you can review and edit it whenever necessary.

Deposits of Goodness

He who has pity on the poor lends to the LORD,
And He will pay back what he has given.

PROVERBS 19:17 NKJV

The Lord is loving, generous, and full of glory. Every good and perfect gift comes from him! When we are generous to the poor, we reflect the nature of our heavenly Father. We don't have to mitigate generosity when every act is like a deposit in a high yield savings account; we get back more than what we put in!

As we trust God to do what is his to do, we get to partner with him in ways that join his purposes to our actions. Our hope is not in money, and it's not in the systems of this world. It is in the character of God who is faithful in mercy and overwhelmingly gracious in goodness. Let's dare to lift our hopes beyond our own little lives while reflecting our beliefs in the ways we choose to live. Generosity is one of the most practical ways to express hope in something outside of ourselves.

When presented with the opportunity, help someone today. Whether it's someone on the side of the road or a mom in the grocery store, be generous and kind.

Reasons to Rejoice

This is the day that the LORD has made.
Let us rejoice and be glad today!

PSALM 118:24 NCV

Every day has within it possibilities for praise. As we look for reasons to be grateful, to rejoice, and to let go of our worries, we join our hearts to the glimmers of hope we find embedded in our lives right now. That awareness serves as a reminder to us to delight and take courage in every one of our experiences. They strengthen our hearts in a confident expectation of the goodness of God. What beauty there is to uncover in even the most ordinary day!

Studies show that our outlooks affect how we will move through our experiences and even how we perceive them. If we carry hope and high expectations for goodness, we will be met with those. If we expect to be disappointed, we will be met with the underlying despair that we carry within us. Our mindsets are so important! We can grow in hope by looking for the glimmers that are already present. The more we attune to them, the more we will notice them! Like a muscle growing stronger, our attention will be directed to the beauty around us.

Take note of every good and beautiful thing you find today, no matter how small. Do this for a week and see if it has made a difference in your outlook.

Power of Friendship

Some friendships don't last for long,
but there is one loving friend who is joined to your heart
closer than any other!

PROVERBS 18:24 TPT

There is evidence that friendship groups significantly affect our psychological and social wellbeing. Social support is important to our emotional and mental health. It is also important for our ability to hope. Hope, as we know already, is an active force which motivates us and clarifies practical steps for us to move toward a goal. When our friends have high levels of hope, it can encourage us on our own. When we go through inevitable dips, the support of friends can help us to persevere.

Good friends truly are a gift from God. Their loving support and honest feedback can keep us from getting too focused on our internal critiques. Being involved in others' lives help us keep a broader perspective as well as enjoy the multiple benefits of physical and social support. It is so important, too, to remember that God is a friend; he knows what others can only surmise. We can trust him to relate to us as someone who loves us thoroughly. His friendship is the firmest foundation of hope that we have.

Reach out to a couple of close friends today and let them know how grateful you are for their friendship.

Listen for It

"Give ear, and hear my voice;
give attention, and hear my speech."

ISAIAH 28:23 ESV

God's Word is full of reasons to hope. It gives a view into who God is. His nature is woven throughout the Scriptures. As we learn to listen to the Spirit's voice in our lives, we find that it is this very character that shines through all of what he says. The Spirit's fruit is the evidence of his work in our lives. As we not only listen to but also apply what the Lord says, we find ourselves on the true path of hope.

Everything God does is with purpose. He uses even what others intend for evil to sow goodness into the lives of those who love him. It's important to recognize his redemption and to know his character. Not everything that happens in life is his will, but he can use everything in his merciful power to bring redemption, restoration, and revival. Let's trust him in hope to do this for us!

Make a list of the attributes of God revealed in Scripture. Meditate on who he is and celebrate when you see his nature in the world around you.

Worthy of Trust

The one who understands a matter finds success,
and the one who trusts in the LORD will be happy.

PROVERBS 16:20 CSB

Trust and hope are deeply connected. The greater the trust
we have in someone, the lower our inhibitions, the greater our
security, and the more intimately we connect with them. When
we feel secure in our relationships, we have no reason to
pretend to be anyone other than who we are. We can be open
and honest, knowing that even disagreements aren't a threat
to our sense of belonging to each other.

More than any other, God is worthy of our trust. He does not
misunderstand, mistreat, or manipulate us. He is impartial,
true, loving, and understanding. What a beautiful friend he is!
As we build trust with the one who never breaks it, our hope
grows to meet the expanse of his trustworthiness. There is
no end to the possibility of growing in hope, for God is ever
expanding in faith!

*Focus on the relationships you have with those you really trust
today and be specific about what you are grateful for in them.*

Alert in Hope

Be on guard. Stand firm in the faith.
Be courageous. Be strong.

1 CORINTHIANS 16:13 NLT

Hope does not deny reality. It does not overlook the challenges in life; hope knows that the rough spots are not the full scope of the story. Anyone who plans for the future and does not make allowances for changes along the way, runs the risk of despairing at the first bump in the road. Making room for the unexpected, allows us to evaluate the next best step when an interruption occurs along the way. Hope faces reality with optimism and a plan.

Courage and strength are hallmarks of a hopeful person. They don't give up easily; throughout life, they can do hard things alongside the delightful things. Hopeful people believe in something greater than themselves. They draw courage from the examples of others; they are willing to be humble themselves, so they are prepared to pivot when something that once worked no longer does. They understand that the journey is as important as the destination. They stand firm in what truly matters and learn to let go of what doesn't. To hope is to build bravery and strength while walking through the twists and turns of this life.

Before you go about your day, decide what is most important to you today. Set an intention and let it guide your choices.

Steps of Wisdom

Be careful how you walk,
not as unwise people but as wise.

EPHESIANS 5:15 NASB

Being intentional with our lives is a statement of hope. Intention in how we interact with others, move along in this world, and work toward our goals are all reflections of the presence or absence of hope.

When we put our hope in God, walking in his wisdom makes sense. He is trustworthy and true, and so are his ways. He wants the best for us, and he knows better than we do about how to navigate both the pitfalls and the peaks of this world. He is loyal in his love and shepherds us with this wisdom. His gospel is simple, and so are his requirements: to love him and to love others. He doesn't require anything that he does not offer us himself. There is grace to make the right decisions, strength to humble ourselves, and peace to calm our fears. He really is the source of every good thing, and his wisdom is worth far more than the wealth of this world!

Is there something in your mind, that you must do, which you haven't acted upon yet? Let today be the day you use wisdom by not delaying any longer. You may find your hope bolstered, as you move ahead.

No Comparison

Each one should test their own actions.
Then they can take pride in themselves alone,
without comparing themselves to someone else.

GALATIANS 6:4 NIV

Instead of focusing on the victories or the faults of others, what if we turned our attention to what it is ours to do instead? When we seek to control others, we lose sight of our own responsibilities and choices. We cannot account for anyone but ourselves. We can offer advice when it is invited; we can support others when they need it. However, the only thing we can actually control is our own actions and reactions.

God is the one to whom we ultimately are accountable. He knows us, and he created us with the unique makeup of gifts, talents, and personalities that we have. From that foundation we can grow in grace, humble ourselves in love, and promote peace in our relationships. This is good work. It's also good work to walk in the liberty of God's love for us! Let's focus on what is ours to do and let go of the need to manage or control others.

Take some time to ground yourself in your responsibilities today. What does God require of you? Put your hope in him and walk it out.

An Acceptable Time

"In an acceptable time I have heard you,
And in the day of salvation I have helped you."
Behold, now is the accepted time;
behold, now is the day of salvation.

2 CORINTHIANS 6:2 NKJV

Hope is important when we create goals. It empowers us to break the processes down into steps to ensure we reach completion. Though we can't just skip the journey to get to the end, we can take actions in consistent ways in our day-to-day decisions. Consistency is key. Intentionality is important. They go together with hope, producing purpose by motivating us toward the goals we set in the moment.

Today is all we have. We cannot put the energy we have today into some other time. We can only embrace the reality of what is true now and then make plans for the future. It is the day-by-day movements we make that produce a life worth living. Our intentions inform our choices. Our choices build pathways into our futures. There's no time like the present, so let's get out of our heads, into our bodies, and do the work that needs to be done.

Make time to either review or set goals that you have for the week, month, or year. Make a plan of execution, breaking down the processes into steps that you can take every day to get closer to the desired end.

Hope in Every Season

Do this because we live in an important time. It is now time for you to wake up from your sleep, because our salvation is nearer now than when we first believed.

ROMANS 13:11 NCV

It is important we are aware of whatever season of life we are in. That way we won't expect to harvest when it's time to plant. The earth and its seasons are cyclical. So is life! One way to harness hope is to take stock of where we are seasonally and what our responsibilities are in that time. Some seasons require more rest or more space. Others require digging in and getting some hard work done. No matter what the season, hope is present in each one.

Our pace of life does not reflect our hope. We don't have to busy ourselves to artificially produce fruit. In fact, it is important we stay focused on the purpose that underlies our work. Otherwise, we may find ourselves working in fields where we don't produce the desirable fruit and we don't even enjoy the work we are doing. We only have so much energy to give, so let's be sure we are putting it where it matters.

Look over the last year of your life. Now consider where you want to be a year from now. In the middle of these two, you will be able to assess where you are. What does this season require of you?

Powerful Prayer

Don't be pulled in different directions or worried about a thing. Be saturated in prayer throughout each day, offering your faith-filled requests before God with overflowing gratitude. Tell him every detail of your life.

PHILIPPIANS 4:6 TPT

Prayerful meditation can decrease anxiety as well as increase hope. As we offer God our worries, we can leave them there at his feet and receive his peace in our hearts. We don't just leave our worries with a random person or simply dump them in some nameless space. We give them to the one who tenderly cares for us. He knows how to take care of us, and he promises to do so! We can be confident in his loyal love and faithful help. His help may not always take the form we prefer, but it is always there.

The practice of prayer can greatly increase our hope both in God and our futures. We shouldn't think that any detail is insignificant to him. He wants us to pour out our hearts to him and to tell him about every detail of our lives. He is good, faithful, and with us through it all. He will never leave us nor forsake us!

No matter how long or short it's been, take time to pray today. Pour out every detail of your life. He loves to know you and for you to know and trust him!

Overwhelming Peace

God's wonderful peace that transcends human
understanding, will guard your heart and
mind through Jesus Christ.

PHILIPPIANS 4:7 TPT

The result of giving God all our worries and leaving them with him is this: God's wonderful peace will be in and through us. As we let him in on every detail of our lives, we no longer carry the burden of them by ourselves. Hope uplifts our hearts and spirits as we place our trust in him. Know that he will guide and care for us with every detail. He is so very good to us!

Hope is creative. It can help us get unstuck. Creativity doesn't have to be found in chaos. It can be found even more readily in times of stability! Science shows that boredom can lead to innovation. Times without a lot of activity can lead to creative solutions and artful problem solving. We need the space that peace brings to truly experience the creative benefits of hope. They can propel us in exciting new ways, even if that entails seeing problems from a new angle.

Instead of filling every moment with stimulation today, set aside at least thirty minutes for quietude—no phone and no music. Let your mind wander. Move your body if it helps. Simply give yourself that free time to experience peace and incorporate it into your life. The benefits may astound you!

Endless Possibilities

"With man this is impossible,
but with God all things are possible."

MATTHEW 19:26 ESV

God is not limited by the things that limit us. Thankfully, he is also not bound by the limitations we place on him. Instead of trying to understand God on our terms, what if we let our imaginations grow to expand every revelation of him? As we embrace the mystery of God and fully realize that he is larger than life and more glorious than we can grasp, we can then imagine a greater God than we currently know. This can help us to grow in faith and hope.

For every problem we have, there is a solution that God's wisdom provides. For every challenge, there is a way through. The one who created all things knows the answers to the questions that we don't even know to ask. This should encourage us in hope and propel us in seeking the Lord with passion. He is accessible, and his power is ready to move in our lives as we lean on him. Even when we experience failure, God has more possibilities for goodness as we follow him!

When you don't know what to do today, ask God for his perspective and his wisdom. Trust that he will help you, and act on his leading.

He Plans It

"You planned evil against me;
God planned it for good to bring about the
present result—the survival of many people."

GENESIS 50:20 CSB

God will not let anything be wasted, not the smallest or the greatest trials in our lives. His mercy sows seeds of hope and his redemptive rain waters them. His grace nourishes the soil and increases the health of the fruit that it bears. We can truly trust him through every hardship. He does not leave us, and he is not finished with us!

If we can imagine the goodness that God has for us, we would never waver in our trust of him. His intentions toward us are full of love: What if we truly believed that? There are ways we can cultivate hope; one of those ways is to listen to words that inspire us to grow and change. Whether it is a sermon, a worship song, or the testimony of someone who walked through hell and came out on the other side, whatever inspires and challenges us is good for our souls and for our hope!

Listen to a motivational speech, an inspiring sermon, or someone's testimony today. When you feel inspired, be sure to write down what it is that impacted you.

A Ready Help

"I hold you by your right hand"
I, the LORD your God. And I say to you,
"Don't be afraid. I am here to help you."

ISAIAH 41:13 NLT

When we know that help is available, hope is not lost. When we feel isolated and alone, it can be easy to drift into despair. It is important to be supported in communities that offer both encouragement and physical help. It is also important to recognize where others fail, God fills in. He guides us by the hand, and he delights in calming our fears with his presence and peace.

Whatever challenges you face today, you have a ready aid! Perhaps you forgot how willing God is to step in and help you. Maybe you've never known that kind of reliance, or it could be that this reliance is what you live with. No matter where you are, God is full of grace to strengthen you in hope and purpose. Whenever you need him, he is there. He won't ever leave you on your own, not even when you find yourself in messes of your own making.

Whenever you are overwhelmed, take a moment to close your eyes, take a deep breath, and imagine God holding your hand. He's got you; he's here to help.

Promise to Sustain

Cast your burden upon the LORD and He will sustain you;
He will never allow the righteous to be shaken.

PSALM 55:22 NASB

What does it mean that God will sustain you? Simply put, he will support and strengthen you spiritually, physically, and emotionally. He is faithful to bear your burdens without buckling under the weight of them. He can handle every concern you have and more. You cannot reach the limits of his love, and you certainly can't reach the limits of his strength. With this in mind, there's no reason to hold back anything from him!

Knowing that God's capacity to bear burdens is exponentially greater than ours, the hope we have in the possibilities of his mercy and redemption can grow. The greater our hope, the more likely we are to act accordingly. Even when we stumble, we will not fall, for God holds each of us by the hand. Every stumble becomes an opportunity to witness God's gracious help. Thank God for his goodness and for his promises which never fail.

Think about what you would do if fear wasn't a factor. Let yourself dream and decide where you want to act.

Rest Assured

We know that in all things God works
for the good of those who love him,
who have been called according to his purpose.

ROMANS 8:28 NIV

Hope is more than a biblical concept. It is a healing tool that harnesses faith and gives an expectation for goodness. It also motivates us to work and inspires change for the better. It has been shown to be an effective intervention for those who struggle with mental health issues, especially in youth. Hope can be a force for change. It is a wonderful reason to rest in the peace of God that comes from trusting him.

The presence of God is filled with his palpable peace. Every time we turn our attention to him, to the goodness of his nature and his overwhelming love for us, our hope can grow. When we are convinced of the power of his love, the lengths that it has gone through and will continue to go through, there is more reason to trust, celebrate, and hope. What a wonderful place of confident rest we find in him!

Do you know someone who struggles to hope for better days? Be intentional in your kindness toward them; a small act of sacrifice, service, or encouragement can be enough to grow their hope even just a little.

Delight in What Is

Enjoy what you have rather than desiring what you don't have. Just dreaming about nice things is meaningless— like chasing the wind.

ECCLESIASTES 6:9 NLT

Comparison can be a trap, and endlessly desiring what we don't have can keep us in a spiral of dissatisfaction. It is much wiser to enjoy what is already ours. Every one of us has reasons to be grateful, and each of us has access to the same sunrise and sunset each day. There is food for our bellies, people whom we care about, and probably a few pleasures that delight us even if those pleasures are not shared by everyone.

Hope not only reaches for what could be true, it embraces and exemplifies what is already true, beautiful, and worthwhile. It may seem counterintuitive to focus on the beauty we already have in our repertoire of experiences now, but if we want to continue to grow in hope, it is important to recognize that the good things we have today also feed our hope for tomorrow. Every bit of goodness is a glimpse into a glorious God. When we waste our time wishing our days away, we miss out on the power of simple pleasures. If we want greater life satisfaction, we choose to be present in each moment.

When you find yourself wishing for something out of reach, reorient your heart in hope by remembering what is yours to enjoy here and now.

February

May the God of hope fill you with
all joy and peace as you trust in him,
so that you may overflow with hope
by the power of the Holy Spirit.

ROMANS 15:13 NIV

Fixed Attention

Holy brethren, partakers of the heavenly calling, consider the Apostle and High Priest of our confession, Christ Jesus.

HEBREWS 3:1 NKJV

When we fix our thoughts on Christ who is our high priest and ultimate teacher, we put him in his rightful place as the leader of our lives. He is the ultimate standard for humans. He is our brother and our friend. He is our Savior. He conquered the grave and offers us the freedom of God's love through his powerful sacrifice. He rose from the dead, was resurrected to life, and so then offered all those who trust in him the same promise of eternal life.

Our thoughts inform our hope. Therefore, when we fix our thoughts on Christ, we center our hope on him. It is good for our hearts to remember who he is, what he has done, and what he promised. He is the author and perfecter of our faith. We rely on him for it all! We partner with his purposes in hope and experience his powerful help because of our relationship with him. This helps us remain strong in hope, and therefore we can cope through the hard times knowing he will not abandon us.

Fix your attention on Christ throughout your day whether you center on him through a song, a passage of Scripture, or a prayer.

Embodied Hope

I rejoice and am glad.
Even my body has hope.

PSALM 16:9 NCV

Knowing we can put our full confidence in God who is faithful, loving, and true, allows us to rest in peace. When we take time to consider how God has faithfully come through for us throughout the previous weeks and years, we can grow in hope for how he will continue to take care of us now and forever.

Embodied hope marries belief and desire. It propels us toward the goals ahead of us. We can tend to downplay the importance of emotions in our logically thinking culture, however emotions give us a lot of information about our wellbeing. We shouldn't be afraid to deeply feel things, for as much as we experience pain, we can also experience joy. As deeply as we feel sadness, we can also experience happiness. We cannot avoid pain and suffering, but we can know peace, joy, hope, and love through it all. There are always reasons to rejoice if we turn our attention to find them!

Every time you experience a reason to be grateful, rejoice, or hope, take a moment to breathe it in and say thank you to the Lord.

Bright Future

Your future is bright and filled with a living hope
that will never fade away.

PROVERBS 23:18 TPT

Having hope gives us both the willpower and the path to get there. Our living hope is in Christ, because even when every other hope fades, he will not. He remains the same yesterday, today, and forever. His pervasive peace floods our hearts as his presence awakens us in hope. As we begin to believe (to really believe) that our future is bright, we move toward that future with a fresh motivation to keep going

We can run the race set before us as Paul described in both 1 Corinthians 9 and Hebrews 12. With eyes fixed on our living hope, we remember what we are moving toward. We see the goal at the end of the race. Life has many obstacles, but it also has many victories. Our bright future remains even in the autumn of our lives, for in Christ we are promised eternal life in his kingdom. What a reason to continue pressing on in hope!

Take a step, no matter how small, toward a hope you hold in your heart.

Hopeful Plans

"I know the plans I have for you," declares the LORD,
"plans for welfare and not for evil,
to give you a future and a hope."

JEREMIAH 29:11 ESV

If the God who created us has good plans for us, then we have no reason to despair about the future. He knows the scope of our lives both in breadth and in the intricacies. There is nothing that his marvelous mercy cannot do for us. He is our Redeemer, restorer, and holy hope. With him, all things are possible.

Instead of becoming overwhelmed by the problems that pop up, what if we changed our thoughts about them? What if we saw them as opportunities instead of burdens? We can practice how we respond, and use what once felt like an inconvenience, as a prompt to go to the Lord for his wisdom. His strategies are better than our responses in most cases anyway. In him, we find encouragement, wisdom, and rest. What a good God he is!

When unexpected things happen today, choose to see how you can be more like Jesus in them, or go to him for help with the answer. He is a ready and close help!

The Kingdom Endures

"In the days of those kings, the God of the heavens will set up a kingdom that will never be destroyed, and this kingdom will not be left to another people. It will crush all these kingdoms and bring them to an end, but will itself endure forever."

DANIEL 2:44 CSB

It can be hard to imagine anything that lasts in a world that is swiftly changing. Day to day, week to week, and year to year, there is so much shifting in our lives and in the world around us. Throughout the ages, kingdoms have risen and fallen. That will continue to be the case. The God of the heavens promises that his kingdom will never be destroyed. It will outlast every other one.

Though for now we only see a reflection, we will one day see the full picture (1 Corinthians 13:12). We will stand face-to-face with Christ. We will live in the fullness of the never-ending kingdom of God. What a powerful hope this is! We don't have to know the full scope of it all and we couldn't understand it if we tried! But one day we will know fully, even as we are fully known.

Work for the things that matter and let go of the things that don't. Consider whether or not you'll care about those things in the future, and if the answer is no, let them go.

Faithful in Small Things

"The master was full of praise. 'Well done, my good and faithful servant. You have been faithful in handling this small amount, so now I will give you many more responsibilities. Let's celebrate together!'"

MATTHEW 25:21 NLT

The one who is faithful with the little things is given more responsibilities. This is true in every sector of society and life. If we are dependable people with our words, following through with our responsibilities, then we will know the honor of being trusted with more. One bright example of this in the Bible is Joseph. Though he was sold into slavery by his brothers, he worked his way up in his master's household by being dependable and trustworthy. It eventually led him to serving the Pharoah with a very high position and a lot of responsibility.

Anyone looking at Joseph's life during that time may have questioned the dream he had when he was young. He foresaw that he would hold a high place of honor. How could a servant, a nobody, get there? God was faithful to Joseph, and he used the painful circumstances of his brothers' rejection to bring him to a place of honor. It was not wishful thinking that got him there but faithfulness to God and the way in which he served with integrity that did.

Be faithful to what is yours to do and watch as your responsibilities grow over time.

No Need to Despair

Hope does not disappoint, because the love of God has been poured out within our hearts through the Holy Spirit who was given to us.

ROMANS 5:5 NASB

Disappointment can lead us to being cautious rather than trustfully leading. Though we will deal with disappointment in our lives, God gives us a hope that will win out in the end. Hope that comes from God will not shift or change even when we do. He always has a good plan. He may take us through dark valleys in life, but God will not let us go. The Holy Spirit is our constant companion, giving us comfort, revelation, and peace.

There is a difference between disappointment and despair. Disappointment occurs when our expectations differ from our reality, and despair is when we lose all sense of goodness with our expectations for the future. We feel doomed, rather than blessed. Thankfully, hope is something that can be cultivated and strengthened. This means that despair can be reversed, no matter how long we have lived with it. God is greater than our feelings, and his wonderful promises will not fail.

Take some time to think about your life and your future. Are there any areas of disappointment or situations when you struggle to hope for better? Ask the Lord to remind you of the power of his faithfulness to you in every area of life and surrender to his love.

Better than Imagined

"What no eye has seen, what no ear has heard,
and what no human mind has conceived"—
the things God has prepared for those who love him—
these are the things God has revealed to us by his Spirit.

1 CORINTHIANS 2:9-10 NIV

We cannot exaggerate the goodness of God! We can't outrun the grace he offers us either. There are fresh mercies awaiting us every morning, and there are opportunities to surrender to his love in every moment. God is near, and the presence of his Spirit empowers us to hope.

Every expression of love we have witnessed in this world is but a small speck of sand in the ocean of his love. We cannot conceive of all that he has planned and has made provision for in the great sea of his mercy and kindness. He is better than we can imagine, and infinitely so! We cannot reach the limits of his love. He is ever so patient with us. How beautiful this truth is! As we truly reflect on the greatness and goodness of God, our hearts soar in hope.

Imagine yourself as a speck of dust and God's love like the air around you. You are always engulfed in it.

Just Like Him

Beloved, now we are children of God; and it has not yet been revealed what we shall be, but we know that when He is revealed, we shall be like Him, for we shall see Him as He is.

1 JOHN 3:2 NKJV

Hope and resilience are the keys to transformation in this life. One day we know that we will be transformed to be Christlike. Until then, we can still partner with his purposes and his nature by becoming more like him through continual surrender as we journey through the ups and downs of this life.

As children of God, we rely on our Father to guide, teach, and correct us. We also depend on him for nourishment, courage, and comfort. His presence helps us remember that we never do anything alone. We don't have to rely on our own strength to get through. This is especially good news in times of utter exhaustion and weakness. He invites us into his rest and offers us peace, joy, and hope. These renew, refresh, and give us what we need to keep going. It is important to remember that we are not loved because of what we can offer, but rather we are loved because of who we are. As we continue to rely on our Father, we can more readily exemplify his loving nature in our own lives.

Whatever you need today, go to the Lord. Spend time in his presence. Meditate on him as your good Father and allow him to reveal himself to you through his Spirit.

What a Day

"He will wipe away every tear from their eyes,
and there will be no more death, sadness, crying, or pain,
because all the old ways are gone."

REVELATION 21:4 NCV

In times of grief, it can be helpful to remember that loss is not something we will always have to deal with. Though there is no shortage of loss in this life, God promises that a better age is on the horizon. In his forever kingdom, there will be no more death, sadness, crying, or pain. Though we weep now, there will come a time when the crying ceases.

Knowing that an end to grief and pain is coming, does it not give us that much more reason to lean into the Prince of Peace here and now? We can know his comfort and peace that passes understanding in the grimmest situation. He calms our nervous systems and brings relief. One day, there will be no more need of relief. But today, we can lean on the one who is near in kindness and ready to comfort us in our grief.

You don't have to deny pain to hope. You can hold both in tension. You can grieve now and have hope for a better tomorrow. Allow sadness, if it is there, and know that God keeps account of your tears.

Power in Forgiveness

Be kind and affectionate toward one another. Has God graciously forgiven you? Then graciously forgive one another in the depths of Christ's love.

EPHESIANS 4:32 TPT

There is so much power in forgiveness. As we let go of the need to control others or their outcomes, we can embrace the love that Christ offers us and offer it to others. What grace there is in this; we forgive because we know what it is to be forgiven. Holding grudges does nothing to harm the person we hold them against, but it does hurt us. Bitterness can cause us to grow cold and indifferent, but forgiveness allows love to melt our defenses.

Forgiveness provides willpower, and that demonstrates the ability to change. This is important to understanding hope; it is tied to it. To hope, we not only have to believe that it is possible, but we also need to take steps toward that end. The ability to change our minds and hearts and to choose to forgive is a powerful way to demonstrate love in action. Forgiveness grows our love for God, for others, and even for ourselves. Forgiveness grows our hope.

Holding on to offenses makes your heart bitter. To grow in hope, choose to let go of your offenses and forgive others. As you go about your day, let go of the things that lead to resentment.

Call to Action

Why are you cast down, O my soul,
and why are you in turmoil within me?
Hope in God; for I shall again praise him,
my salvation and my God.

PSALM 42:5-6 ESV

Hope is perhaps the only positive emotion that requires the presence of a negative one to be activated. Uncertainty can create the need for hope to spring into action. Without a challenge present, hope is not necessary. However, we know that there are a multitude of opportunities to practice this.

The presence of a challenge is a call to action for hope. Hope is creative, and it can offer innovative solutions. We might not have seen some of the possible steps we can take if not for the particular challenge we are now facing. Thankfully, God is the ultimate problem solver. He doesn't always step in and sweep us up and out of our circumstances. In fact, most often, he shows us the way through. Hope is the light that signals us forward. Thank God for the power of hope!

Remember throughout your day that every challenge is an opportunity for hope. Repeat today's verse whenever you need that reminder.

Effects of Hope

Gray hair is a glorious crown;
it is found in the ways of righteousness.

PROVERBS 16:31 CSB

A long life is a blessing. Hope can make our lives rich with wisdom as we keep our hearts entwined with the love of God. As we journey through this life with the Spirit as our guide, we walk in the ways of God's righteousness. The expectation of goodness keeps our hopes high even as we deal with the struggles of humanity.

Not all of us will grow old, but we can all know the power of God's faithful love guiding us in hope. Research shows that the effects of hope are more than emotional. It can improve our physical health, our relationships, and the quality of our sleep. Overall, hope enriches the lives we lead and is a worthwhile trait to cultivate and strengthen.

Science shows that hope can have a positive impact on your health, your relationships, and your outlook. Consider where you are today and what your challenges are. Use those as a reason to practice hope and keep choosing to move toward it.

Ways of Thinking

"Just as the heavens are higher than the earth,
so my ways are higher than your ways
and my thoughts higher than your thoughts."

ISAIAH 55:9 NLT

Hope offers us a different way to think about a situation. It offers a perspective that is higher than the human frustrations of the moment. Having true hope can lead us out of areas where we feel stuck. In fact, studies show that our physical systems can also be positively impacted. Hope can change our bodily systems which are stuck in malfunction or illness by offering a different focus and a healing pathway.

Hope allows us to believe that there is a different possibility. There are options outside of those we already know; we just may not be aware of them yet. God is infinite in his wisdom. He is never at a loss for what to do. Perhaps the thing we need most when we are in a situation that needs problem solving is hope. Instead of looking to simply make the problem better, ask the one who is higher than us to offer a different perspective. That may be just what inspires us in hope.

When you aren't sure how to move forward today, ask the Lord to give you a different perspective about the specific area in which you feel stuck.

It Matters

You have taken account of my miseries;
Put my tears in Your bottle.
Are they not in Your book?

PSALM 56:8 NASB

God's gracious comfort meets us in our messes. It meets us in the devastation and the grief. He takes notice of every tear that falls. We are seen and known by the Creator of the universe. He not only celebrates our wins, but he weeps in our sorrows. We cannot find a better friend. He does not tell us to get on with our lives when we can't get out of bed because of grief. He comes in close with comfort, reassurance, and rest. He will not let us go. Not ever.

If it matters to you, beloved, it matters to him. God doesn't overlook the desires of your heart. In fact, Psalm 37:4 says, "Delight yourself in the Lord; and He will give you the desires of your heart." He cares what you care about. Give him your worries, rest in his comforting peace, and allow him to speak words of encouragement to your heart. He is your hope, and your hope will not fail.

Instead of denying your emotions, invite God into them. Ask him to meet you where you are at today.

Gracious Hope

With minds that are alert and fully sober,
set your hope on the grace to be brought to you
when Jesus Christ is revealed at his coming.

1 PETER 1:13 NIV

We live in the tension of the "now but not yet." We are saved now but still in need of saving from the constant troubles in life. We are forgiven now but still in need of forgiveness. We are healed now but are still holding out for healing. We are alive now and yet we wait for the eternal life promised through Christ. Can we hold the tensions of this life with hope?

There is so much freedom in Christ, and yet we are still shedding layers to become more liberated in God's love. We can journey through this life with hope and still be aware that our hope will be tested. We can change our minds at any moment. We can walk with the confidence of God's grace which is meeting and empowering us no matter where we are or what we do. He really is that good. What a hope we have in him!

Be gracious and compassionate with yourself and others today. When your hope is tested, find your rest in God who offers absolute peace. It's okay to take a break and start over again.

Shared Comfort

Blessed be the God and Father of our Lord Jesus Christ, the Father of mercies and God of all comfort, who comforts us in all our tribulation, that we may be able to comfort those who are in any trouble, with the comfort with which we ourselves are comforted by God.

2 CORINTHIANS 1:3-4 NKJV

Every time we experience the comfort of God, we have more experience to draw from so we can extend comfort to others. When we reach out in compassion to those who are hurting, we reflect on the love of God which is alive and well in our hearts. When we choose to stay at a distance from those who are hurting, it can reflect a lack of care or proper concern. Let's be sure to let love lead us and allow our hearts to open even if it calls to mind our own pain.

When someone tries to comfort us, it is an encouragement and an acknowledgment that we are seen, known, and loved. The comfort of God is tender. It's gentle. It doesn't demand anything in return. It is freely offered and full of peace. What hope we can feel when comfort meets us in such an act of pure kindness.

If you see or know someone who is struggling today, take time to offer them a kind gesture. It may be just the thing they need for their hope to be rekindled.

No Condemnation

Those who are in Christ Jesus
are not judged guilty.

ROMANS 8:1 NCV

Shame can leave us feeling overwhelmed and hopeless. It tells us that we are worthless. This can lead to feelings of despair which has us thinking we should give up. Shame keeps us stuck in spirals of self-destruction. God never shames us. Guilt does have its place, though. It points to an area where we have missed the mark. Perhaps we have hurt someone. What we do with this guilt determines how we will proceed. If we ask for forgiveness and make amends, we are free to live in the restoration of that act. If we refuse to acknowledge our part in someone's suffering, we ourselves may suffer even more afterwards. Guilt says we've done something wrong. Shame says there is something wrong with us. There is a difference.

If we struggle under shame, it will be hard to have hope. However, when we dare to see ourselves from God's perspective, we are challenged to think differently. Christ offers us freedom, not only from sin, but also from condemnation. He is a liberator and a benevolent grace giver. Let's drink deeply from his fountain of grace today.

Ask the Lord to show you areas where you may be mired by shame but where he wants to set you free.

Incomparable Glory

I am convinced that any suffering we endure is less than
nothing compared to the magnitude of glory that is about
to be unveiled within us.

ROMANS 8:18 TPT

Hope is a powerful coping tool. It can help us get through
really hard times. When our focus goes beyond the suffering
in the moment, we are reminded that this difficult time is not
the end. Suffering and pain are not all that exists, and it won't
last forever.

Nothing can compare to the glory that will be unveiled
through God's work in our hearts and lives. It is always better
than what we can imagine. Every trial is grounds for goodness.
Every problem is a possibility for a deeper experience with
God's love, peace, and wisdom. He is faithful to help us
through every issue. If you have thought about coping skills as
a negative necessity, think again! It is how we survive. Hope is
a wonderful tool, and it gives us the motivation to persevere
when we might otherwise give up.

Strengthen your ability to hope by reminding yourself of
God's presence, his help, and his promises every time you feel
tested today.

Think About It

The LORD your God is in your midst,
a mighty one who will save;
he will rejoice over you with gladness;
he will quiet you by his love;
he will exult over you with loud singing.

ZEPHANIAH 3:17 ESV

The power of God's love for us can restore our souls and renew our minds as we experience it. In fact, even simply thinking about his love can impact us greatly. Meditation is found throughout Scripture. The psalmists illustrated the power of meditating on God's Word and his attributes. When we are challenged by life, choosing to take the time to think about what God promises and who he is, can boost our expectations, uplift our hearts, and strengthen us with hope.

Hope is a way of thinking. This is paramount for us to understand. We can grow in hope as we turn our thoughts toward God's love for us which is lifegiving. When we turn our thoughts to our beautiful God who is in our midst and who rejoices over us with gladness, we are encouraged by his presence, his thoughtfulness, and his care for us. He loves us so well! As dearly loved children, we can trust his faithfulness in every moment and situation.

When you are tempted to worry today, turn your attention to how much God cares for you.

Brilliant Light

The LORD God is a sun and shield.
The LORD grants favor and honor;
he does not withhold the good
from those who live with integrity.

PSALM 84:11 CSB

In the brilliance of God's perfect nature, we can see more clearly. Though there are many challenges in this life, happy is the person who trusts in the Lord of Armies! If we live in the light as he is in the light, we have nothing to hide. Integrity keeps us honest and honorable. Even when we fail, if we trust in God, we can humble ourselves and admit our wrongdoings. We are more willing to seek repentance and restoration. We choose to do good in love. We learn from our mistakes and grow in compassion for others. We live within the liberty found in love, and we have nothing to fear.

How we live matters much more than what our vocations are. Little things done with love are as important as great things done in service to an ideology. In fact, the impact of small things may outlast the results of grand schemes. Those who live with integrity choose to do the right thing, even when the right thing isn't popular.

Take a good look at your lifestyle and mindset. How does integrity play a role? How much does love lead? Ask the Holy Spirit for help in aligning with his kingdom's ways.

Trust Him

Trust in the LORD with all your heart;
do not depend on your own understanding.
Seek his will in all you do,
and he will show you which path to take.

PROVERBS 3:5-6 NLT

It is so very important that we recognize we do not know all there is to know. In fact, we are each far from the fullness of wisdom. As long as we remain open to continuously learn, are willing to readjust as necessary, and stay humble before the Lord and others, we will be able to expand in wisdom and hope as our understanding grows.

Too often, when we form an opinion about something, we can dig in our heels instead of listening to other viewpoints. We must lean on God for understanding. Just because we have understood something one way does not mean that it is how God sees it. We must separate our opinions from God's wisdom. We must be humble in our hearts and minds and allow him to correct us and grow our compassion. Trust and hope are inextricably linked. If we trust that God knows best, when he gives us greater revelations, hope lights the path forward.

When you think you know best, ask the Lord for his wisdom to shine through your own. Be willing to pivot when you find his perfect perspective supersedes your own.

Merciful Beginnings

The LORD's acts of mercy indeed do not end,
For His compassions do not fail.
They are new every morning;
Great is Your faithfulness.

LAMENTATIONS 3:22-23 NASB

If we did not think that there was a chance to start afresh in our relationships, careers, or any area of life, what hope would we have to grow and change? Hope requires both belief and desire. When the day is long and we are burdened by the weight of the world, the knowledge that tomorrow is another day to start fresh can bring both peace and hope. If we believe that we can lay down our burdens and receive the mercy of God to refresh our hearts and our visions, then we have the desire to take steps to bring us closer to these things. We have hope.

There is never a moment when we are without the mercy of God. Sometimes the one thing we need to do the most is rest. We need to lay down the need to do one more thing and simply be still; we need hearts that are prepared to receive. This is not laziness. We were made to exist within the rhythms of rest. The endless guilt motivation to be productive robs us of the great gift of peace which comes when we truly let ourselves recharge.

Schedule time to rest or to simply let yourself off the hook today without adhering to an agenda; do what feels restful, so you rejuvenate your body and mind.

Choose Love

Do not destroy the work of God for the sake of food.
All food is clean, but it is wrong for a person to eat
anything that causes someone else to stumble.

ROMANS 14:20 NIV

Just because we feel righteous with our opinions doesn't
mean we should flaunt them in front of those who disagree
with us. We can stay true to our convictions and yet
remain kind toward others by not doing that which may be
controversial in front of them. There is a time and a place for
challenging others, but when it comes to the non-essentials
of the faith, the one who practices love chooses the right path
regardless of the details.

The issue of clean and unclean foods is an important one in
the Jewish culture. Of course, Paul knew this. He encouraged
those who felt free in their consciences to eat whatever
they wanted to do so, but he also encouraged them to not
let that decision be a stumbling block for others. This kind
of sensitivity is a loving act. We can choose behavior that
is different from others and still be culturally and socially
sensitive to those people. The greatest lesson here is to do all
things in love. This may sound simple, but it can be a radical
act of love.

*When presented with the opportunity to either be right or be
kind, choose kindness today.*

Actively Content

Let your conduct be without covetousness; be content
with such things as you have. For He Himself has said,
"I will never leave you nor forsake you."

HEBREWS 13:5 NKJV

Contentment, just like hope, requires active engagement. It
doesn't happen by accident. It is developed by appreciating
what we have. Gratitude practices can aid in growing our
satisfaction with life. Trusting the Lord for our provisions also
helps us be content, especially as we witness how he has
already provided and will continue to do so in the future.

When we are focused on what others have that we don't,
we leave ourselves open to jealousy. When we lay down
any comparisons, we can focus instead on the gifts already
present in our own lives. God is present in our lives. He is living
and active, and his power moves in miraculous ways. Our
lives may look different than we expected, but that doesn't
mean that they aren't filled with beautiful fruit. Let's take
time to cultivate the ground of our own lives and appreciate
what is already ours, trusting the one who never leaves us nor
forsakes us and who will continue to do great things.

*Write down everything you can think of in your life that you
are grateful for. Work on focusing on the good you have
rather than on the enticing things that others have.*

Fountain of Hope

I pray that the God who gives hope will fill you with much joy and peace while you trust in him. Then your hope will overflow by the power of the Holy Spirit.

ROMANS 15:13 NCV

The evidence of trusting God is found in the hope we have in our hearts. The good news is that we don't have to strive or reach for this encouragement. Even a small turn of our hearts toward him is met with the overwhelming goodness of his presence. He has so much joy and peace to offer us. He is overflowing in wisdom and love. He gives hope as freely as a well-fed spring of water offers refreshment. He is the source; he is pure, generous, and infinitely better than we can imagine.

Hope is needed when challenges come our way. It keeps us moving forward. It gives us a goal to reach for, while also fueling our creativity by motivating us to see things from a different perspective. When we are running low on hope, we can always go to God who gives freely from his fountain of grace. All we need is found in him. Hope is a gift of resilience, and it will not fail us.

Take time in prayer to tell the Lord why you trust him. Give him specific scenarios and people. Choose to trust him with them.

The Pressure Is Off

No one will ever be able to boast, for salvation is never a reward for good works or human striving.

EPHESIANS 2:9 TPT

We are saved by grace which does not come from us. It is a gift from God! We could never earn it, and in the same way we need not fear losing it. We each have a destiny. He created us in love, covering us with the power of Christ's death and resurrection. His life is now our hope. His redemption has made us new, and it will continue to do so!

Knowing that we can't earn God's grace, we can let go of the need to prove ourselves by simply responding to him in the liberty of his love. He is so gracious in kindness. He is so patient in mercy. Though we are accustomed to striving and trying to be as perfect as possible to appear good, God doesn't require this. He wants to give us rest in his mercy. He wants to renew our hearts in the peace of his gracious gift. What would you do if you knew the pressure to perform well was always off?

Instead of working toward whatever you think you need to, consider what it is you want. There is room in God's grace for your heartfelt desires!

A Vision

"Every place that the sole of your foot will tread upon
I have given to you, just as I promised to Moses."

JOSHUA 1:3 ESV

After Moses died, Joshua took his place as the leader of Israel.
The Hebrew refugees had not yet entered their Promised
Land. They needed direction; they needed a leader who
would guide them in the ways of the Lord. Joshua was fearful,
however. That is why God told him more than once throughout
the book of Joshua to be strong and courageous.

God spoke about courage to Joshua, but he also gave him a
clear vision to walk toward. That was the hope that Joshua
needed. It was not merely vague encouragement. It was a
tangible reassurance of God's presence and what he promised
to do through Joshua. In the same way that God offered
Joshua hope through a vision, he does the same in our own
lives as he gives us a hope to walk toward.

*Do you have a promise of God or a clear desire and belief for
something that seems out of reach now? Let hope guide you
and give you a strategy as you break down the steps needed
to get there. If that seems too overwhelming, just start with
the first step.*

March

Faith is confidence
in what we hope for
and assurance about
what we do not see.

Hebrews 11:1 niv

Encouraging Fruit

Hope delayed makes the heart sick,
but desire fulfilled is a tree of life.

PROVERBS 13:12 CSB

Some hopes do not take long to appear in our lives. A little bit of work, a little of life, and there they come as natural as the sunrise. Others, however, are harder won. But even the most out-of-reach hope has a pathway that leads to it. We simply must see the steps we can take and consistently do what is ours to do. Remember, hope is active. It is not a mere wish. It is a way of thinking that propels us with perseverance.

A tree offers sweet fruit when it is ripened right on the branch. The satisfaction and sweetness cannot be overstated. It is delicious, refreshing, and enjoyable. This is what it is like to experience a long-awaited desire coming to fruition. Don't worry, God has not forgotten you or your desires. Take heart and continue to trust him.

It is easy to overlook the fruit in your life which is the result of what you once longed for. Do you see the fruition of a hope you once held? Take some time to thank God for those blessings. Out of your gratitude and satisfaction, remember that he who provided will continue to be faithful.

Free from Fear

I prayed to the LORD, and he answered me.
He freed me from all my fears.
Those who look to him for help will be radiant with joy;
no shadow of shame will darken their faces.

PSALM 34:4-5 NLT

Research shows that fear can keep people and even whole societies in cycles of conflict. If we want to show peace in the way we promote it as well as how we submit to it, we cannot let fear override hope. Thankfully, we have help. Though humans are quick to engage with fighting, God is patient in love. He offers us freedom in this mercy. Our nervous systems are equipped with fight, flight, or freeze responses. These are activated under different kinds of threats, but even the fear of a threat can cause one of those responses to flare.

The peace of God brings clarity and calmness to our nervous systems and minds. There is space in love to slow down and breathe. Fear pushes us to protect ourselves in rash, sometimes counterintuitive ways. The peace of God allows us to make wise decisions as we realize that we are safe. If we want to walk in the power of hope, such crippling fear must be overcome.

Is there an area of your life in which you cannot think clearly with an open mind or heart? Perhaps fear is keeping you stuck. Ask the Lord for his peace and for his wise perspective.

Comfort for Anxiety

If I should say, "My foot has slipped,"
Your faithfulness, Lord, will support me.
When my anxious thoughts multiply within me,
Your comfort delights my soul.

PSALM 94:18-19 NASB

Our psychological wellbeing is as important as our physical health. Our quality of life is intricately interwoven with our outlook on everything. Even during times of physical stress, we can learn to cope and heal by strengthening our hope and optimism. This isn't the same as positive thinking. Hope is linked to real possibilities. We can accept that we are suffering while also being hopeful for the future.

Anxiety can be debilitating. It creates persistent and intense worry and fear about everyday situations. Though anxiety can be normal in stressful situations, it is an entirely different matter when it overtakes one's everyday life. When we trust God to take care of us, and we realize that no challenge is too big that can't be overcome with his help, we experience the lifegiving hope which his comfort brings. The delight and relief are sweet. God's presence brings comfort to all who look to him for help.

Be intentional about your mental wellbeing today. If you are overwhelmed, take care. Spend time with the Lord. Take a walk in nature, have a shower, or give someone a hug. These small, comforting acts can do wonders for your outlook!

Powerful Peace

"I have told you these things,
so that in me you may have peace.
In this world you will have trouble.
But take heart! I have overcome the world."

JOHN 16:33 NIV

Jesus did not promise that we would experience pain-free lives. In fact, he guaranteed that we would know trouble in this lifetime. He warned his disciples about coming hardships because he didn't want them to be taken off guard by them. The same is true for us. If we go through life expecting ease, we will become discouraged at the first sign of trouble. However, even in the troubles of this life, we can know the all-surpassing peace of Christ. He has overcome the world, and in him we have an overwhelming hope.

Challenges are an opportunity to practice trust, receive peace, and harness hope. Every trouble presents us with possibilities. We should never hold God to a standard of a mess-free life for his children. He never promised that, and we will never have it. He did promise to be with us through it all, though. There is powerful peace in his presence which calms every fear and gives us strategic hope to hold on to.

Endeavor to see every frustration, trouble, and challenge today as an opportunity to practice peace and to lean into wisdom and hope from God.

Satisfying Portion

"The Lord is my portion," says my soul,
"Therefore I hope in Him!"

LAMENTATIONS 3:24 NKJV

Hope grows in a well-nourished heart. When the Lord is our portion, we have everything we need for life and godliness, including hope, itself! Second Peter 1:3 says, "His divine power has given to us all things that pertain to life and godliness, through the knowledge of Him who called us by glory and virtue." His divine power offers us love, joy, peace, patience, kindness, self-control, and hope.

The Lord is our source of every good thing. Every deficiency we have is healed and nourished by his presence. Whatever it is we need, he has it. Let's begin our days with his presence and end each evening with gratefulness. Every time we have a need, let's ask the Lord to provide for it, and then remember to rejoice when he does so. He is our satisfying portion. We can hope in him!

Hope helps you look for solutions here and now. When you have a need, go to the Lord with it. Ask him to provide the solution and to open your eyes so you can partner with his purposes in hope.

Hopeful Action

God did not give us a spirit that makes us afraid
but a spirit of power and love and self-control.

2 TIMOTHY 1:7 NCV

Hope is active. When we have a goal, we practice self-control
and ambition toward that end. When we see the pathways to
get to where we hope to go, we are engaged with this active
hope. Hope doesn't take away our power to partner with God
to achieve it. It empowers us, giving us a spirit of power and
love and self-control.

If our hope doesn't produce within us the desire or the
motivation to do what is necessary to get there, it is more
like a wish. God doesn't want us to stay stuck in fear, whether
it is a real threat or simply us engaging with the unknowns
and the what ifs. He wants us to move in the liberty of his
love, empowering us in self-control, and choosing that which
aligns with his kingdom. It is a beautiful thing that we have the
power of freewill and his love!

*Self-control is a vital part of moving ahead with hope. You
cannot have it all, do it all, or expect things to magically come
together out of thin air. Your work is paired with God's grace,
and it is a powerhouse of hope for that reason. Prioritize your
forward movement today, even if that means saying no to
other things.*

Inspiration and Encouragement

Whatever was written beforehand is meant to instruct us in how to live. The Scriptures impart to us encouragement and inspiration so that we can live in hope and endure all things.

ROMANS 15:4 TPT

The wisdom of the Scriptures and the example of others who walked the path of faith is a living demonstration of God's faithfulness. It can be encouraging and inspiring to our own walks of faith to hear of others who have gone before us. If we want to live in hope and do well enduring the pitfalls of life, reading the Word is important. If we want to know God better, one of the best ways to do it is through the inspired revelation of his character and person in Scripture.

When we are discouraged, it can be tempting to have a pity party. We may feel alone in our struggles. However, there are so many stories in the Bible that can teach us and encourage us. The psalms are filled with the breadth of human experience. We are not alone in our struggles, and we are not unique in them either. Everyone struggles! This is why looking to heroes of hope can help us. Our own hope can be built by hearing the testimonies of others who have struggled, endured, and triumphed. Scripture is filled with them!

Pick a Bible story or a couple of psalms to read today. Look for God's light and the breakthrough moments. Be encouraged.

In the Shadows

Even though I walk through
the valley of the shadow of death,
I will fear no evil, for you are with me;
your rod and your staff, they comfort me.

PSALM 23:4 ESV

We cannot avoid the valleys in this life. Some are darker, longer, and bumpier than others. We cannot wish ourselves out of them. The losses of life hit especially hard. We know certain grief eventually comes but we really can't prepare for that. Even so, we are not alone. When we cannot see past the end of this moment, the end of this hour, when our sadness is like a heavy fog, even then our Good Shepherd guides us. His comfort is near.

Hope doesn't have to feel happy, and it isn't a guarantee. It can be enough just to remind us that after the long, dark night, the light of morning will dawn again. We travel through the dark valley, but it is not where we build a home. We will see the open expanse of fields and sky once more. Until then, we lean on the guidance of the one who always sees us clearly. He holds us close.

If you are having a hard time hoping in big ways, hope in small ways. Perhaps, the promise of a new day is enough for you today.

Empowered to Continue

I am able to do all things
through him who strengthens me.

PHILIPPIANS 4:13 CSB

In the verse before the one above, Paul declared, "I know how to make do with little, and I know how to make do with a lot. In any and all circumstances I have learned the secret of being content." We can do all things through the one who strengthens us. We can learn contentment in any and every situation by his grace. We don't have to wait for our circumstances to align to know peace, hope, and joy. We can experience them here and now no matter what our lives look like.

This is a powerful principle that we must not ignore! In God, we find strength to enjoy our lives and enjoy him throughout. We also find strength to continue with purpose and clarity. If God is our reason to live with integrity, then we always have it. He promises to help us whenever we cry out to him. There is power to do all things through Christ who strengthens us from the inside out!

Not everything others expect of you is necessarily something you should do. You need to be clear on what your purpose is and go from there. Evaluate your responsibilities and see if there are any that don't align with who you want to be or what God requires of you.

Various Expressions

The same Spirit gives great faith to another, and to someone else the one Spirit gives the gift of healing.

1 CORINTHIANS 12:9 NLT

Each of us can hope in ways that are as varied as our personalities. There is a reason God made us so wonderfully diverse! He is a creative God, and he delights in our unique expressions. Though many systems are threatened by differences, and many seek to uphold sameness as an ideal, this was not true of Jesus. He offered the values of God's kingdom for us to live by, but he did not speak about the specifics of how we should dress, what music we should prefer, or any other details of individual personalities and choices. It is important to cultivate God's values. Cultures are diverse over time and people groups, but God's values are timeless.

We all have different preferences, gifts, and talents. This reflects a God who delights in our diverse expressions. Throughout creation we see the creativity and playfulness of a God who doesn't even repeat snowflakes which each are distinct in their pattern. Instead of fearing what makes each of us different, let's learn to delight in it! Love binds us, but it doesn't erase who we are.

Dare to be unashamedly you today. Let the virtues of Christ compel you, but don't judge outer appearances, not even your own!

Confident Expectation

The Lord is my light and my salvation;
Whom should I fear?
The Lord is the defense of my life;
Whom should I dread?

PSALM 27:1 NASB

We already know that hope is necessary because perfection isn't reality. No one can ever find a perfect life! This is why it can be such a trap to compare our struggles with the highlight reels of other people. Even those who seem to be living a dreamy life have their struggles. We don't know their obstacles. As we direct our gazes toward our own lives, we may at first find reasons to fear: an impending procedure, a burdensome bill, or an unknown outcome may threaten our peace. Still, the Lord is with us. He is our light and our salvation.

Let's not let our gazes stop at the details of our lives. Let's be sure to lift them to the one who created us in love. With God as our defense and our shield, we don't have to give in to fear. In fact, the pervasive peace of his presence fills our souls and hearts with hope as we meditate on his faithfulness. He is ever so near, and what leaves us breathless doesn't startle him one bit!

You don't have to avoid your questions to know peace. Offer them all to God in prayer and ask him to light up your heart with hope and the reality of his nearness.

Necessity of Faith

We live by faith,
not by sight.

2 CORINTHIANS 5:7 NIV

Without faith, we have no hope. Faith allows us to see what is not yet and take steps toward that objective to make it a reality. Faith is the belief in something we cannot see, and hope is the desire that marries with that belief to create a way forward. One day hope and faith will have no purpose because we will see all that remains unseen to us now. If we are living on this earth in this one short life, faith and hope together are our motivation!

We don't have to prove our hope right now. It requires faith because whatever it is that we hope for does not yet exist in our lives. While we can ground ourselves in contentment, hope is necessary to keep us moving forward with intention and purpose. Faith in God, in his ability to change us, and in the power of his nature continues to keep us moving forward. Hope allows us to not see what is in the future yet know that our faithful God does.

Faith in God can help us hope and therefore keep moving forward. What connections do you see between your own belief and the hopes you have?

Fulfilled Hopes

You have turned for me my mourning into dancing;
You have put off my sackcloth
and clothed me with gladness.

PSALM 30:11 NKJV

When we experience the relief our hearts long for, it can feel overwhelming. When David penned Psalm 30, it was from a place of thanksgiving and praise for God coming through for him. He cried out to the Lord, and in return, he received help.

These moments of relief, wonder, and rejoicing are like bookmarks for our faith. We can draw fresh hope from them as we remember what God has done for us before, apply it to our present troubles, and then hold great hope for the unknowns of the future. No matter what comes, God is with us. He turns our mourning into dancing, and we rejoice in the relief of his great power and love!

Think back to a time when you felt like a burden had been lifted from your shoulders. What did that relief mean to you? Garner strength from that experience and let it boost your expectations of God's continued faithfulness.

Priorities

Love the LORD, all you who belong to him.
The LORD protects those who truly believe,
but he punishes the proud as much as they have sinned.
All you who put your hope in the LORD be strong and brave.

PSALM 31:23-24 NCV

It is no small thing to center our lives around loving the Lord. Jesus said it best: "Love the Lord your God with all your heart, all your soul, all your mind, and all your strength" (Mark 12:30). When we set our priorities on loving God well with our whole beings, everything else falls into place. With our hope set firmly on him, on his faithfulness and his loyal love, we can continue to grow in grace each day.

Again, Jesus said, "Seek first God's kingdom and what God wants. Then all your other needs will be met as well" (Matthew 6:33). When we focus ourselves on pleasing God by living according to his purposes and values, we set up every other area of our lives for success. If we set our priorities straight in him, we will have the clarity of hope to keep us aligned in Christ's kingdom ways.

Consider three practical ways you can prioritize loving the Lord in word and deed, then be sure to incorporate them into your life.

Continuous Connection

Let joy be your continual feast. Make your life a prayer.
And in the midst of everything be always giving thanks,
for this is God's perfect plan for you in Christ Jesus.

1 Thessalonians 5:16-18 tpt

In every season, no matter how full or how empty, there is a reason to feast on joy. Consider the Israelites when they were in the desert. God gave them manna from heaven to nourish their bodies, yet it was nothing like the milk and honey they dreamed of in the Promised Land. Even so, in the desert they had reasons to rejoice. God had miraculously provided food for them. We also can find joy in God's simple provisions, not only in the obviously abundant seasons.

The Israelites had the presence of God leading them in the barrenness of the desert. God was present in a cloud by day and a pillar of fire at night. In our wilderness seasons, God's presence is with us, too. As we make our lives a continual prayer, we find ways of connection to the ever-present one who never leaves us nor forsakes us. He may not always appear in the same way, but that does not mean he is not with us. Let's lean into our connections with him by way of an open heart which feeds on the hope he offers.

Keep an open line of prayer going throughout your day. Every time you receive some provision from God, no matter how small or large, give thanks and take joy.

Testing

Count it all joy, my brothers, when you meet trials of various kinds, for you know that the testing of your faith produces steadfastness. And let steadfastness have its full effect, that you may be perfect and complete, lacking in nothing.

JAMES 1:2-4 ESV

Discomfort is not a feeling most of us welcome, however, it can produce growth if we let it. James said that the testing of our faith produces steadfastness. Steadfastness, which is the ability to endure, is strengthened as we persist through challenging times. Perseverance doesn't often look like happiness in the moment, but we can still understand the fruit of joy in the work it takes to keep going.

The full effect of remaining steadfast in trials of various kinds is the perfecting of our characters until we are complete and lacking nothing. This process is an ongoing one which we won't give up until Christ returns. Still, this means every trial is an opportunity to grow in all that we are called and created to be. How beautiful that Christ refines us through the fires in the trials of life. Nothing goes to waste in his love!

Sometimes to endure well, you need a physical outlet. Do something physically challenging or emotionally engaging regularly to help relieve the stress that builds up.

A Help Up

The LORD helps all who fall;
he raises up all who are oppressed.

PSALM 145:14 CSB

There is always a reason to hope with God. The story never ends with defeat or shame. There is promise for resurrection, restoration, and revival. Though the old may pass away, the new will come. Those who fall will be lifted up. It is so different from what the world is constantly communicating. Even what seems doomed to us holds within it the promise of hopeful recovery or a fresh beginning if we look through eyes of hope. *The Lord helps all who fall.* No one is out of his reach. Nothing is too overwhelming for his power to overcome.

If you find yourself in need of help today, don't be discouraged. God is a faithful provider, and he knows just what you need. Lean on him and let him lift you up from the ground if you have fallen. You are as loved in your failures as you are in your victories; don't ever forget it!

Don't let despair (about anything!) keep you from trusting the Lord for breakthrough. He always has a way out, and his arm is strong to save. Put your hope in him!

Keep Moving

The righteous keep moving forward,
and those with clean hands become stronger and stronger.

JOB 17:9 NLT

Hope is not an emotional high. It isn't endless happiness.
It is the vision of possibility that brings clarity and craving
together. With desire to see our hopes as motivation, we
walk in the faith that the hope is not only possible to achieve,
but an eventuality. Faith and works go together, and this
perhaps is revealed most acutely in hope. Belief activates us in
movement.

The invitation to keep moving forward is not a mandate for
burnout. Movement can look different from day to day. It
can be a small step one day and a mile the next. Don't be
discouraged if your journey seems to be slower than someone
else's. Your life is unique, and so is your path. Your talents and
your challenges will also be different. Slow movement is still
movement.

*Consistent small steps forward are shown to lead to long term
success. Considering this, set an intention to take small steps
toward your goal. Don't forget to include a day of rest!*

The Kindness of Favor

May the kindness of the L<small>ORD</small> our God be upon us;
And confirm for us the work of our hands.

P<small>SALM</small> 90:17 <small>NASB</small>

There are some miracles we hope for that we can do nothing about. We can only ask and trust that the Lord will come through. Other times, our hopes are contingent upon the work we do. Thankfully, the Lord blesses the work of our hands as we submit our ways to him. When we walk in the integrity of his kingdom's ways, we have nothing to fear. When we live open-heartedly before him, we may fall many times, but every time we will get up in the grace he offers and start again.

God is so kind to us. He is gracious in love and generous in provision. He does not wish us harm but good. That is why he tells us the best way to live! We can choose our own path, but his wisdom supersedes our own. Through reliance and time (and trial and error), we will find this to be true. Though the systems of this world are rigid, God's kindness is fluid. How beautiful to know that we can find our home in him! He will guard, teach, and refine us, even as he puts his generous favor on the humble offerings we make.

Take stock of your driving influences and be sure that they are aligned with how you actually want to live. What you pursue can define or refine you.

Wholehearted Hope

Whatever you do, work at it with all your heart, as working for the Lord, not for human masters, since you know that you will receive an inheritance from the Lord as a reward. It is the Lord Christ you are serving.

COLOSSIANS 3:23-24 NIV

If we do not know what we are working toward, we may get lost in the day-to-day tasks that seem urgent but aren't beneficial. This isn't to say that we deflect our responsibilities. But if we let the urgent overtake the important things, we may end up remaining stuck rather than moving forward.

Not every important task will be what we want to do. Yet, each is needed to make meaningful progress. No matter what industry we are in, we will only feel the satisfaction of a job well done if we feel like we are making progress in ways that truly matter. Hope is paramount to keeping our perspective right and bringing clarity to the important things we can do right now. Those steps may not seem beautiful or noteworthy, but they are what are necessary. Whatever we do, no matter how humble, let's do it with all our heart, *as if we are working for the Lord*.

Look ahead to the next couple days (or week) and determine the most important priorities and tasks. If it is too much, consider what you can delegate and what you can do yourself. Be intentional about getting these things done.

Resist the Urge

Do all things without complaining and disputing, that you may become blameless and harmless, children of God without fault in the midst of a crooked and perverse generation, among whom you shine as lights in the world,

PHILIPPIANS 2:14-15 NKJV

We know that hope begins with our perspectives. If that is true, our attitudes play into this, too. If our expectations around others and ourselves become burdened with complaints and disputes, we may be too distracted by the blame and pride that arises to focus on the things that matter. Division can bring destruction, but overlooking an offense is to our honor. Paul warned in Romans 16:17, to "note those who cause divisions and offenses, contrary to the doctrine which you learned, and avoid them." This isn't speaking of a careless word or complaint, but of an attitude of offense that does nothing but divide.

On the contrary, when love is our goal, we can do as Proverbs 17:9 says: "Love overlooks the mistakes of others, but dwelling on the failures of others devastates friendships" (TPT). Hope sees possibilities where hyper focusing on others' faults can breed discouragement.

Instead of arguing with someone who has a different point of view today, choose to simply love and live your life. Do what is yours to do, and let others do the same.

Walk in the Way of Hope

Happy are those who respect the Lord and obey him.
You will enjoy what you work for,
and you will be blessed with good things.

PSALM 128:1-2 NCV

Hopeful people are not reckless. They don't do whatever they want, whenever they want to. They know the power of self-control and the wisdom of focus. They recognize that regulation now can lead to success later. Being goal directed helps hopeful people to keep in mind what is important and what is also non-essential.

God's Word and ways have so much wisdom to direct us. Even within our own hopes that don't seem to directly link to the Lord, he offers us the *way* to walk and the values to incorporate. God's nature is exemplified in Scripture much more than any physical description of his person. In the same way, it is our nature, the way we choose to live and treat others, that will stand the test of time. We can be disciplined and glorify God with our priorities. We can be diligent and make time for people. The way of hope may not be linear, but it is filled with good things.

Consider both what you can reduce your time and resources on that distract you from your goal, and how you spend your time on the things that matter.

Placed with Purpose

Yahweh-God took the man and placed him in the garden of Eden to work and watch over it.

GENESIS 2:15 TPT

Every person has a purpose. Even from the beginning, God set Adam in the garden to work and watch over it. Before Adam even knew the meaning of life, he was given a job and a purpose. We each have our own responsibilities that are uniquely our own. No one is without God's purpose for them. And it is not a burden! It is what we were created for. Work is a part of being human, as important to us as eating, breathing, and resting. It is not all we are created for, to be sure, but it is a powerful part of it.

We have an off-balance relationship with work in the West. For too many of us, our jobs become a part of our identities. Adam's identity was not as garden watcher. It was simply something he got to do. He was created as a friend of God, and he got to walk with him in the cool of the day. Let's not get caught up on the specifics of our work or how it may reflect on us. We can simply do the work as part of what is natural to us, and commune with our God who helps us in every way.

What is your relationship with work? Ask the Lord to reveal where you may need more balance, both in your approach and your expectations.

Abundance Is Available

If any of you lacks wisdom, let him ask God, who gives generously to all without reproach, and it will be given him.

JAMES 1:5 ESV

Our expectation can dictate our willingness to reach out. This is as true with God as it is with others in our lives. If we know that God's resources are abundant and he generously offers what he has to those who ask, then there is no reason for us to struggle on our own. We don't have to be afraid of his reception. Even when we are unsure, when we ask, we will find that we are met by his generous kindness!

Hope can thrive in secure relationships. These are the kinds of spaces where we are met by love and understanding. Even when we disagree, there is quick restoration. There is humility. There is dependability. There is reciprocation. May we have these people in our lives, and may we be them!

Think of the reliable and welcoming people in your life, the ones you know you can always count on and who love you as you are. Thank them for being who they are to you and be sure to be specific!

A Renewed Mind

Do not be conformed to this age, but be transformed by the renewing of your mind, so that you may discern what is the good, pleasing, and perfect will of God.

ROMANS 12:2 CSB

There is transformative power in the renewal of our thinking. When we see from a different perspective, new neural pathways form in our brains. It is both a biological and cognitive shift, and it can do wonders for our understanding and expectations. If we believe everything that the world tells us, we will conform to a chaotic and small-minded worldview. It is good to challenge our thoughts and hold them against the Word of God. Discernment doesn't happen by accident. It takes intentionality to see from different perspectives and to remember who God is in all of it.

At any point, our minds can be renewed. The systems of this world do fail and will continue to. However, God's kingdom will remain. It is so important that we keep our focus on the things that truly matter, then, and give ourselves to them. As we do, not only will our minds be transformed, but our entire beings will also benefit.

Pay attention throughout your day to see where your mind wanders or the thoughts you have in reaction to news. With this awareness, ask the Lord to show you where you can renew your thoughts in his wisdom.

Spoken Life

If you are wise and understand God's ways, prove it by living an honorable life, doing good works with the humility that comes from wisdom.

JAMES 3:13 NLT

Our choices reflect our beliefs, and our lifestyles reveal what is important to us. If we want to walk in the wisdom of God, we must do more than get acquainted with it. We must put it into practice. Wisdom is not proud or brash; it's not immovable. Humility is as much a part of reflecting God's wisdom in our lives as any other trait, so let's be sure to keep our hearts open and teachable before him.

Proverbs says a lot about the fool. One of the ways that we can spot a foolish person is the way that they talk like they know everything. If they are unwilling to admit their own shortcomings or gaps in understanding, they are not wise at all. Pride goes before a fall, and they, indeed, will fall. The way we live our lives says more about us than our status or appearance. Let's make sure that what our lives say about us is what we want remembered of us!

Hope is intentional. Look at what your life, your relationships, especially, says about you. What do the people you work with say? What would your family say is important to you? Make the necessary adjustments where you recognize a difference in what you want and what is true.

Ever Expanding

This I pray, that your love may overflow still more and more
in real knowledge and all discernment.

PHILIPPIANS 1:9 NASB

Just as the love of God is limitless, so are the possibilities
hidden within it. Where there is love, there is hope for
restoration. There is hope for peace. There is hope for joy.
There is hope for redemption and renewal. Love isn't simply
a concept; it is the power of God! We can expect to continue
to expand and grow in God's love as he empowers us in grace
every time, we come to him.

It is not naïve to practice hope. In fact, it is small-minded to
believe that our perspective of the future doesn't matter.
Where we may tend to stay small, God is inviting us into a
larger understanding. His love is expansive; our experiences
of it are just a blip in its great expanse. Why, then, would
we seek to stay small (or comfortable) in our understanding
and expectations, when there is an invitation to *overflow still
more and more in real knowledge and all discernment*? We
cannot reach the end of it, so let's embrace the journey and
be the sojourners we're meant to, letting each new experience
broaden our horizons and enrich our lives!

*Where have you been "playing small" when it comes to your
belief systems and lifestyle? Don't let fear hold you back from
learning and experiencing the more that God has for you.*

Draw Near

Let us then approach God's throne of grace with confidence, so that we may receive mercy and find grace to help us in our time of need.

HEBREWS 4:16 NIV

There is no need to stay away from God not for any reason! Even when we feel the weight of our guilt, he waits with mercy to cover us as we approach him. There is grace to empower us in our weakness. There is abundant kindness to wash away our fears. There is peace to calm the chaos of confusion. All that we need is in him!

God does not wait like a panther ready to pounce on those who pass by him. He is more like the father of the prodigal son, looking and waiting for his children to turn to him as he runs out to meet each one! He will never condemn us when we humble ourselves before him. Even his correction is laced with kindness. Let's go to him, then, no matter how little or long it has been. His reception will love us to life all over again, as he covers us in the robes of his mercy and refreshes our hope in the comfort of his arms!

Spend intentional time in the presence of God throughout your day, turning your attention to him whenever you think of it.

Confident Assurance

This is the confidence that we have in Him, that if we ask anything according to His will, He hears us. And if we know that He hears us, whatever we ask, we know that we have the petitions that we have asked of Him.

1 JOHN 5:14-15 NKJV

Needs are not weakness. It is impossible to be human and not be needy. Check in and see how that statement sits with you. Are you resistant? You may think that you are strong, but there is no need to be strong all the time. You may be incredibly resilient and have made do with what life has thrown your way, but that does in no way mean that you are not without need and that those needs don't matter. They do, and so do you.

Even if all you can do today is ask the Lord to meet your needs, it is enough to admit that you have them. He is a good Father, and he will provide for his children. You can count on him! Let his faithfulness set the tone for your expectation. He has not overlooked you, and he sees what others do not. He knows your longings and the care that you should have received, even if you didn't. Let him minister to the parts of you that need a nurturer, a provider, and a defender. He has got you!

Set your expectation on God, even if you feel confident in your own abilities; they will fail you at some point. Ask the Lord for his perspective and his grace.

Power of Acceptance

"I tell you to believe that you have received the things you ask for in prayer, and God will give them to you."

MARK 11:24 NCV

Part of the reason why confidence so greatly affects our hope is because it also moves us into action. If we pray to God, believing that we have what we ask of him, we then act like those who will receive it. This means that we do what is ours to do; we partner with the purposes of God and make steps in the direction of our hopes.

Having faith in God does not start and end with our minds. It isn't a vain wish. Yes, there is power in our mindsets, but God's faithfulness is our measure. He is greater than our faith. We are constantly growing in our ability to understand the ways of God, and as we do, we accept his purposes. As we do this, the foundation of our faith grows strong and from there we can build our lives according to the blueprint of hope. When our foundation is strong, everything else benefits.

Ask the Lord for help when you need it and believe that you have it. As you recognize his great grace, allow yourself to move ahead with confidence, knowing he will do what you cannot, but that you can work without fear, as well.

No One Excluded

Most of all, I'm writing to encourage you to pray with gratitude to God. Pray for all men with all forms of prayers and requests as you intercede with intense passion.

1 TIMOTHY 2:1 TPT

There are some situations and people that seem unreasonable to hope for transformation. It is not our job to control people—not in the least!—but we can certainly pray for God's powerful love to take care of them and transform them. What seems unreasonable to hope for in our own strength is an opportunity to intercede and increase our faith in God to do the impossible. When we pray the best for others, we will also do our best to help when we can.

Keeping our hearts open and active in compassion is a good way to stay connected to others. Prayer is a powerful and effective tool to do just that. Instead of remaining indifferent to others' needs, we can pray for them. As we pray for them, we also may be activated in hope to intervene. However, even if all we do is intercede with love, God honors that and does even greater things than we could imagine. Let's stretch our hearts and attention by being purposeful in prayer, especially for the people we are naturally quick to judge.

Practice turning your judgments into prayer and allowing God to soften your heart as you ask for his best over the lives of others.

April

In this hope we were saved,
but hope that is seen Is not hope,
because who hopes for what he sees?
Now if we hope for what we do not see,
we eagerly wait for it with patience.

ROMANS 8.24-25 CSB

Set Up for Success

Where there is no guidance, a people falls,
but in an abundance of counselors there is safety.

PROVERBS 11:14 ESV

If we want to stay strong in our hope, the encouragement and perspective of wise counselors can help us. Whether close friends, mentors, family, or experts in their field, a variety of perspectives can keep us balanced. While our choices are ours, weighing the input of others can be extremely helpful in making those decisions and in seeing steps and paths we may not have on our own.

Truly, if we want to be successful, we must do the work, but we also must remain open and teachable. If we are able and willing to pivot when presented with a better way when our own isn't working, we choose wisdom's ways. Hope may give us motivation, but the counsel of others will help refine the way we go.

Consider one hope you have in your life that you are wanting to put more action behind. Seek out counsel from different perspectives and make note of the advice that you want to incorporate. Don't rely on forging a new path alone when there is wisdom available from those who have gone before to inform and help you!

What You Wish For

"Whoever wants to become great among you
must be your servant."

MATTHEW 20:26 CSB

Humility is non-negotiable in the kingdom of Christ. We are not to lord our positions over others or misuse our power. When we remain focused on our own interests and serve them alone, we choose poorly, and we certainly don't put the love of God at the forefront of our lives. A humble heart knows how to love well, but a proud one remains resistant to change.

If Christ calls us to follow his example in love, we cannot maintain an air of indifference to those who are suffering. If we want to be *great*, we must be willing to serve others well. The best kinds of leaders are those who don't delegate everything, they're the ones who lead by example.

If your hopes include any level of leadership, you must be sure to prioritize service to others and to keep your heart humble. No task is beneath a person who is committed to serving and loving well. Choose at least one way to serve someone in your life today in a practical way.

Doing Better

"Someone who does not know, and then does something wrong, will be punished only lightly. When someone has been given much, much will be required in return; and when someone has been entrusted with much, even more will be required."

LUKE 12:48 NLT

When we don't know better and we make mistakes, we can learn from the correction offered. However, when we keep making the same mistakes repeatedly, it is more than a simple mistake. There must be willingness to change, trying to do better. Maya Angelou famously said, "Do the best you can until you know better. Then, when you know better, do better."

Hope is an anchor for the soul, but it is not immoveable. It keeps us tethered so that we won't aimlessly wander, offering us steadiness when the winds would make us drift. When we try our best and fail, realizing that there is a better way, hope helps us to pivot rather than give up entirely. The way we go about living is more important than the particulars, for our values motivate our actions.

Instead of getting down on yourself for a mistake today, try to see it with neutrality. Mistakes are not indictments of our character, but opportunities to grow in character.

Humble Heart Posture

> Through the grace given to me I say to everyone among you not to think more highly of himself than he ought to think; but to think so as to have sound judgment, as God has allotted to each a measure of faith.
>
> ROMANS 12:3 NASB

A humble heart keeps us open to transformation and change. When we can admit our shortcomings, we can also strengthen those areas of weakness by choosing differently. Humility keeps us honest with ourselves, others, and God. The humble are willing to see from different perspectives and to treat others with kindness and respect. Surely, our heart postures matter in how we interact with others, and God honors those who do the work of humbling themselves before him.

The well-known Proverb warns against protecting ourselves in pride: "Pride goes before destruction, and a haughty spirit before stumbling" (16:18). The unwillingness of the proud to admit that there may be another way may just be the thing that causes them to stumble. Let's be sure to keep our hope grounded in the power and goodness of God, not in our vain attempts at control.

Be kind and gracious with the people in your life today, recognizing your own need for understanding from others.

Unseen Connections

In him we were also chosen, having been predestined according to the plan of him who works out everything in conformity with the purpose of his will.

EPHESIANS 1:11 NIV

Before we knew to choose to follow God and his wonderful ways, he chose us. Before the foundations of the earth were laid, God chose us in love to be his. This is almost too much for us to comprehend. The Creator of the universe, and all that it holds, was thinking of us before he said, "Let there be light."

Just because we don't see the connections of how things work together on the surface does not mean that they aren't there. We cannot see the wind, but it moves both waves and wheat; it affects both the clouds and trees. Think of the electrical grids within our cities. We cannot see every cable or how it is wired into every building, and yet the networks are detailed and empowered by their connections. God does this even more through his creative design in our lives. His mercy weaves in ways that we cannot detect, and yet we see the effects in our homes and lives! What a powerful confirmation of our hope!

Ask the Lord to reveal connections of mercy and hope in your life that are evidence of his faithfulness. Share what he reveals with someone you trust.

All Accounted For

"Are not two sparrows sold for a copper coin? And not one
of them falls to the ground apart from your Father's will.
But the very hairs of your head are all numbered. Do not
fear therefore; you are of more value than many sparrows."

MATTHEW 10:29–31 NKJV

The level of hope we have does not depend on our adverse
experiences; it relies on the support present within our lives.
Even knowing that we are seen, known, and loved in our
hardships can be all the difference. Support offers safety and
relief. It helps us develop resilience.

If a sparrow's plummet to the earth does not escape the
notice of God, we can rest assured that he doesn't overlook
us in our need. Jesus said, the very hairs of your head are all
numbered. God knows your quirks and coping mechanisms.
He is faithful to help you, and he is also faithful to put people
in your life to depend on. You are worth far more than a
sparrow to him, so don't be discouraged. Instead, look to
where support is already available. That is evidence of God's
care for you!

*Instead of depending on solutions to problems to gain a
sense of relief today, find it instead in the safety net of your
friends and family: the solid supports that you can rely on
when you need help.*

Origin and Source

Through his power all things were made—
things in heaven and on earth, things seen and unseen,
all powers, authorities, lords, and rulers.
All things were made through Christ and for Christ.

COLOSSIANS 1:16-17 NCV

Research has shown that belief in God and activity within a spiritual community is associated with higher levels of hope. Hope is not uncertain or vague; it is specific, but still unique to each person. For those facing unknown health outcomes, hope is especially important.

When we put our trust in a greater source, namely, in the one who created all and who cares for all, it can be extremely beneficial to our hope to share this belief with others who do the same. God knows us in and out, through and through. He knows the possible outcomes of every factor, and he guides us in his wisdom and love as we rely on him. God's power knows no limit, and so can our faith in him. Let's trust him with the unknown, for he is competent, caring, and always moving in the power of his mercy.

Connect with someone who you know as an encouragement to your faith today. Share something you're hoping for and offer to pray for what they may be holding out for, as well.

First Chosen

In love he chose us before he laid the foundation of the universe! Because of his great love, he ordained us, so that we would be seen as holy in his eyes with an unstained innocence.

EPHESIANS 1:4 TPT

The hope we have in Christ cannot be overstated. His kingdom holds more goodness and an incredibly richer experience of life than we could ever imagine. It is not about what we earn, accomplish, or collect. It is in the power of the fruit of his Spirit that we find fulfillment and satisfaction. God, in his great love, chose us to be his own before we were formed in the womb. How, then, do we act as those who have chosen to love and serve him in return? By making his values our own and submitting to his ways.

Galatians 5 tells us what the fruit of the Spirit is. This is how we recognize that God is working in and through us. These values are meant to be limitless, so they are more than a safe bet to commit to incorporating in our lives. What practical hope there is in a life partnered with the Holy Spirit!

Pick a fruit of the Spirit to focus on incorporating in your life more intentionally and focus on practicing it every day for a week.

Courageous Confidence

Christ is faithful over God's house as a son. And we are his house, if indeed we hold fast our confidence and our boasting in our hope.

HEBREWS 3:6 ESV

Courage is required to follow the Lord wholeheartedly. This is because, though God can see the end from the beginning, we cannot. Sometimes, we will simply have to trust him as we do what he has called us to do, perhaps without the clarity of what the consequences will be. We may not know how every act of obedience to his ways will play out, but we can certainly trust the nature of the one who calls us.

It is so very important to cultivate a deeper connection with the Lord. The more we get to know what he is like, the more we know what to expect of him. As our expectations grow and align with his kingdom ways, we don't need the assurance of specific outcomes anymore; we are able to trust that the faithfulness of God covers what we cannot expect. We can take courage, as Joshua had to do many times over. We can trust in the help of God, as David also had to do in times of trouble. Courageous confidence takes active faith tied to fierce hope, but we can strengthen it with each step of faith we take!

Choose courage in the face of the unknown today by remembering the hope to which you were called as God's child.

The Greatest Standard

When God made a promise to Abraham,
since he had no one greater to swear by,
he swore by himself.

HEBREWS 6:13 CSB

God has no need to swear by the things we can see. He is stronger than the fiercest army. He is more powerful than the most influential leaders of the world. What he says goes—every time. Though he does not always intervene in ways we wish he would, he does promise to help every time we need it. His promises are his oath, and he will not revoke them. We can recall and recite them as often as we need to encourage our hearts in hope.

God, knowing that we need reassurance, doesn't withhold his encouragement from us. He knows how easily we falter and how quickly we forget. He generously offers us grace upon grace and limitless mercy. We can find all that we need in him, and we can trust him to be faithful, even to the end.

Whenever you need some reassurance today, ask the Lord for some. Choose a verse or a promise to recite when you need a quick shot of encouragement. After all, his Word is living and active!

Meaningful Work

Be strong and immovable. Always work enthusiastically for the Lord, for you know that nothing you do for the Lord is ever useless.

1 CORINTHIANS 15:58 NLT

Even our day-to-day tasks, when done with love and intention to those around us and unto the Lord, are meaningful to him. Choosing to follow Christ's lead in our lives always leads to kingdom fruit. It may not seem exciting to others, but the work that is ours to do, right here and now, is nonetheless a meaningful way to live, serve, and love him well.

If all we ever appreciated were the exciting things in life, we would miss out on the power of simplicity. There is peace in a simple life. There is joy in a job well done. There is satisfaction in knowing we've done our best. Let's not give up, then, especially when it comes to the small, consistent steps that move us further to reflecting God's faithfulness and mercy in our lives.

Let yourself get enthusiastic about your day! Even if it feels silly, hype yourself up for the small things, as well as the things you maybe don't enjoy. Thank God for the gift of ability and for the opportunity to experience him in every aspect of your life.

Doing Good

Who is there to harm you if you prove zealous
for what is good?

1 PETER 3:13 NASB

Passionate devotion to doing what is right and good, the
things that please the Lord, is a powerful way to live. While
some may be passionate about the particulars of their lives,
what if we got passionate about the way we live? What if we
were serious about serving? What if we were incessant about
kindness? What if we were overboard in generosity? This kind
of passionate devotion would display the kingdom of Christ
alive and working in our hearts.

Whatever our hopes are, we must learn to push past fear.
Worrying about what others may think of us, how we might
be received or perceived, is a waste of energy. That isn't to say
that we shouldn't consider our impact; of course we should
be mindful. But when it comes to doing good, there is no
law. Let's not stop ourselves from outlandish love by talking
ourselves out of it for fear of what others may or may not
think of us. Love is a propeller, so let's stop resisting it and
instead go with it!

*Think about how you want to be known. What are the values
you want to shine through in your life? Choose to fearlessly
align your decisions, both big and small, with them today.*

It All Counts

God is not unjust; he will not forget your work and the love you have shown him as you have helped his people and continue to help them.

HEBREWS 6:10 NIV

God has a perfect memory. He sees clearly into the future, too. You can trust that he won't forget a single movement you've made in mercy. He won't overlook your sacrifices of love. He sees, he knows, and he holds on to them.

Even when we forget the good that we've done, God doesn't. It's not that he's keeping score, because what matters is the motivation behind our actions. He sees our hearts, as well as our challenges. He knows our desires and the fears that keep us from moving toward them. It is not necessary for you to keep count of it all. You can trust him. Ask for his help. Rely on his guidance, and he will lead you in his wisdom. He won't let you fall, and he won't trick you. He is always good, always kind, and always wanting the best for you.

Ask the Lord to remind you of an impactful time in your life where you relied on him, and he showed himself to you. Commit to love him, others, and yourself well through the work you do and the trust you show in his faithfulness.

Promise for Renewal

Those who wait on the LORD
Shall renew their strength;
They shall mount up with wings like eagles,
They shall run and not be weary,
They shall walk and not faint.

ISAIAH 40:31 NKJV

God does not promise that we will never grow weak or hungry in this life. However, he does promise to feed us and to renew our strength in his presence. He is a great provider. If we weren't going to experience need in this life, there would be no value in knowing him this way. However, we all know what it is to be exhausted. We all will know the grief of a broken heart and the disappointment of a broken dream. It's impossible to have it all, here and now. But God promises to renew and refresh us, to revive us in hope and to give us fresh vision.

If you find yourself in need of strength, wait on the Lord today. If you find yourself in need of *anything*, in fact, wait on him. His grace will empower you. His presence will pervade you with peace. He will comfort, guide, and encourage you. Go to him as often as you need; there is no limit to his listening abilities or to his welcome of you!

Pinpoint an area of your life where you need some renewal.
Ask the Lord to meet you in that place.

Everlasting Love

These three things continue forever: faith, hope, and love.
And the greatest of these is love.

1 CORINTHIANS 13:13 NCV

The three things that will last into eternity, according to 1 Corinthians 13, are: *faith, hope, and love*. The greatest, and what we know as the overarching nature of God through various expressions, is love.

Love is not only the foundation of God's character; it is how he reveals himself in the world around us. Every act of love is an expression of his presence in that place and time. If we choose the loving thing, no matter what that is, we choose to be like God. There is, then, no excuse for our hatred or offense. There is no rightful reason to be stingy or cold. If we choose to walk in the way of love, we lay down the need to explain ourselves. Let's align ourselves in love, and faith and hope will also be tied to our actions.

Lay down every excuse you have to refuse kindness to others today, and choose to outdo yourself in love, even when it is a sacrifice to do so.

Faithful Foundation

Wrap your heart tightly around the hope that lives within us, knowing that God always keeps his promises!

The faithfulness of God is dependent on his character, not ours. 2 Timothy 2:13 encourages us, "But even if we are faithless, he will still be full of faith, for he never wavers in his faithfulness to us!" God is true and trustworthy. He won't ever wander from his own ways or turn back from his nature. He is the same God who told Moses, "I am who I am" in Exodus 3. The God who was, who is, and who is still to come will never change. He won't go back on a single promise that he has made!

It can be an incredible relief to know that God's goodness does not depend on our own, as well. He is merciful, kind, just, and true. He cannot stop being himself. So, trust him, you, his child! Take hope in who he is and what he has promised. He is a firm foundation, rock steady and a safe place to land.

Wrap your heart tightly around the hope of Christ by offering him your trust. Choose to give him your worries and leave them there. He is faithful to come through!

Necessary Patience

If we hope for what we do not see,
we wait for it with patience.

ROMANS 8:25 ESV

Patience isn't just a virtue, as we've heard. It is an important aspect of hope. We grow in patience as our perspectives broaden. The things of life that are most valuable require a level of patience to produce. Relationships deepen with time, effort, and context. Character is produced through the tests of life. Precious jewels are formed in the dark, with pressure and time. When we realize that time is not our enemy, we can utilize the time we have with a hopeful perspective, the motivation to do the work that is ours today, and garner patience to produce results.

The promises of God, as the Word of God says, are "yes and amen" (2 Corinthians 1:20). Even so, they are not immediate. There is support in the here and now. We have provision for our needs in the one who fathers us with tender care. We have the powerful presence of God, even as we work and patiently wait for what is still to come.

Patience is possible to cultivate. Make a choice to slow down in your day and take time to put your hope into perspective.

Holistic Hope

I wait for the LORD;
I wait and put my hope in his word.

PSALM 130:5 CSB

In the space between petition and answer, promise and fulfillment, there is an opportunity for wholehearted waiting. We can actively wait for God to come through for us as we hope in him. How do we do this well? It may look different from day to day, but it will always be a mix of surrendered trust and courage to face what comes.

As our whole beings expect God to break through for us, we put our hope in him. We can still face the day, along with its challenges, wholly trusting the Lord to do what he alone can do with the offering of what little we can do in partnership. Remember the widow's offering in Mark 12? It was nothing to others, but it was a huge sacrifice to her. Give what you can, and God will bless it.

Do what you can do today, offering what little it may seem, and trust God with the rest.

Powerfully Good News

The Spirit of the Sovereign LORD is upon me,
for the LORD has anointed me to bring good news to the poor.
He has sent me to comfort the brokenhearted
and to proclaim that captives will be released and prisoners
will be freed.

ISAIAH 61:1 NLT

The Good News of the Gospel is exceedingly hopeful for all who know the limits of their humanity. The poor feel their need acutely. They cannot choose to buy or do whatever they want. They must make hard decisions. They may rely on help from others, in fact, because they don't have enough on their own. This does not make them less than. It makes them a target for God's overwhelming goodness!

The happy don't need comfort, and the free person doesn't need liberation. When we recognize our lack, we make room to receive from God's great grace. As we partner with him in hope, his gracious love becomes motivation to see others through the lens of his compassion.

Every area of need is a powerful place of promise that God wants to step into with his grace. Rejoice, then, as you bring God your needs, and leave your worries with him. Be generous with your abundance, and willingly share with those who have less than you. You reflect God's abundant grace when you do!

Reason to Celebrate

[Love] does not rejoice in unrighteousness, but rejoices with the truth; it keeps every confidence, it believes all things, hopes all things, endures all things.

1 CORINTHIANS 13:6-7 NASB

Love is at the root of all that we hope for and all that we do. Love is the very essence of God, and its power cannot be exaggerated. Where there are expressions of love, there is reason to celebrate. We don't have to wait for a big day or milestone in life to choose to rejoice. We can celebrate the little things, as well as the big. It may just be the fuel our hope needs to grow and stay strong.

When we look with intention for expressions of love in our lives and in the world around us, we will find them. Every act of kindness and compassion is a meaningful commemoration of love. They are worth celebrating, even if our rejoicing doesn't leave our own hearts in the moment. A stranger helping a vulnerable person across the street, a neighbor offering to mow the lawn, a coffee covered, undivided attention, these are all reasons to rejoice, for they are all expressions of love. Our hope grows in the soil of love, so let's be diligent about tilling that soil.

Look for little ways to show kindness, compassion, and understanding throughout your interactions today.

Careful Persistence

We want each of you to show this same diligence to the very end, so that what you hope for may be fully realized.

HEBREWS 6:11 NIV

Diligence can make or break our goals. If we don't have the follow through to keep taking small steps forward, we won't see progress. If we expect our hopes to be realized without any effort at all on our part, we will be sorely disappointed. True hope acts as a motivator to move ahead in practical ways toward the hope we have.

Major change can be made by a little bit of work with a lot of consistency over time. Water can erode stone over time. There may be little noticeable difference in days, months, and even from year-to-year, but over decades and centuries, the effect of water's consistent work makes itself evident. The same principle is true in our lives. Though we may not see a huge change from one day to another, with consistent effort, we will see the transformation when we look back to where we started.

Put a plan in place toward a hope you have and do a little bit every day (or every week) toward that end. Consistency always pays off!

Don't Give Up

Let us not grow weary while doing good,
for in due season we shall reap if we do not lose heart.

GALATIANS 6:9 NKJV

If we believe that our efforts don't make a difference, then we will have no reason to keep doing them. Motivation may get us started, but if we don't remember the purpose behind it along the way, we may lose sight of why we even took it up or wonder if our efforts are worth it. Belief in what we hope for, along with the desire to reach it, will keep us going. And when we lose motivation, perhaps what we need is a refresh, whether through the act of remembering why we started in the first place, evaluating whether it's what we still want, and by long to the stories of perseverance in others' lives for encouragement.

Giving up is not in and of itself a bad thing. If we find that what we are doing is no longer aligned with our values, it is okay to redirect. No matter the kind of good we do in this world, if we keep moving in love and purpose, we will reap a harvest when it is time. More than anything, how we go about living, even more than the particulars of what we do, will reflect in the fruit of our lives.

Is there an important hope you have that has been stagnant for a while? Consider how you can take one small step toward it today.

Set the Direction

Be careful what you think,
because your thoughts run your life.

PROVERBS 4:23 NCV

Our mindsets really do matter. How we think about things will affect how we choose to interact with them. Our thoughts direct us in our choices. It's so important that we not let fear dictate our lives. It's incredibly valuable to redirect our thoughts when they are leading us down a road of despair. How we do this may look different, but some wonderful ways to do this include spending time with people who are hopeful and have a positive outlook on life, listening to things that inspire us, and engaging in a community that both supports and challenges us.

We can't overlook what we spend time consuming, for what we ingest affects the direction of our thoughts. If we are constantly watching the news, with little else to balance it out, it may have us expecting the world to fall apart at any moment. If we spend most of our time with people who complain and compare themselves to others, we tend to do the same. Be intentional with what and who you surround yourself with, and take a break to engage with peace when you need it.

Check in on your thoughts throughout the day. What do they reflect? Where do you think they stem from?

Now and Not Yet

With all that you have to look forward to, may you be eager to be found living pure lives when you come into his presence, without blemish and filled with peace.

2 PETER 3:14 TPT

As children of God, we are invited to dwell within the presence of God. He is the source that fills our cup to overflowing. He offers us all that we need through the grace of his Spirit. As we actively engage with the Spirit life within us, we yield to his leadership and his ways. His love is a banner that flies over our hearts, and in the lifegiving atmosphere of his delight, we know the peace of his presence.

There is so much to look forward to, knowing that God is faithful, merciful, and true. He is just and kind. He is a powerful savior and overwhelmingly reliable help. Even as we look forward to what is to come, we can dwell in the rich peace he offers us today. Every moment is a possibility for expansion in love. We can do both: hope for what will be and delight in what is available to us now.

There are so many tensions that you can hold at the same time. Consider how you can both trust for better and delight in what is good, here, and now.

Searching Over

Whoever diligently seeks good seeks favor,
but evil comes to him who searches for it.

PROVERBS 11:27 ESV

Though optimism can be an incredibly powerful trait, unrealistic optimism is the false belief that one is less likely to experience a negative life event. The fact is that we all will experience hardships in this life. We will each know pain, loss, and grief. This is not being a downer; it's simply true! Even Jesus warned his disciples against the notion that they wouldn't experience challenges. In fact, he told them that they unequivocally would!

There is a difference between hope and blind optimism. Hope can handle the challenges that come and be flexible in the face of them. It is creative and persistent. It does not equate challenge with failure. Blind optimism refuses to admit that there is a possibility for hardship, which can lead to more pain. The principle is true that you'll find what you search for. If you look for ways to do good, you will find them. If you look for opportunities to cheat, you will also find those. If you search for reasons to be grateful, you will discover them. If you search for ways to do harm, you will also discover those. Wisdom allows for reality while also motivating us in the possibilities that remain.

You can train your heart in hope, and you don't have to dismiss the hard things to do it!

Clear Directives

"Determine in your mind and heart to seek the Lord your God. Get started building the Lord God's sanctuary so that you may bring the ark of the Lord's covenant and the holy articles of God to the temple that is to be built for the name of the Lord."

1 Chronicles 22:19 csb

There is hope in this passage of Scripture. Can you spot it? It is the hope of a temple of the Living God: a dedicated space where the Spirit would dwell, and the people would come to worship. What is particularly impactful about this hope isn't just that it *could* exist, but that the Israelites would partner with God to *build it*.

What hope have you been given that you need to build toward? Taking it from theory to a blueprint is the difference in an ideal and a plan. There was hope for a dedicated place to honor the Lord and his presence, but there was also a plan. What is it that you need to get started building today?

Hope without a plan isn't hope at all; it's just a wish. Spend time drawing out an outline, or a list of things you can do to move toward building your hope. What is the next step? Perhaps it's simply to start. Whatever it is, take it seriously and do the work!

Be Intentional Today

> "If you carefully obey the commands I am giving you today, and if you love the LORD your God and serve him with all your heart and soul, then he will send the rains in their proper seasons—the early and late rains—so you can bring in your harvests of grain, new wine, and olive oil."
>
> DEUTERONOMY 11:13-14 NLT

When we begin our day with the intention to love the Lord our God and serve him with our whole hearts and souls, we set the foundation for choosing his ways throughout our day. There is nothing we go about, no area of our lives, that are outside the realm of his love. Every choice that reflects his nature is one that honors him.

Our God is gracious. He is more generous than we give him credit for. Instead of limiting what he can do, let's venture to grow in hope, peace, and love. Let's allow joy to motivate our hearts. He delights when we move in mercy, as he moves in mercy. He honors the work we do that no one notices. He sees our intention and our follow through. Let's live for him and his gaze today!

Spend some time in the presence of the Lord, grounding yourself in his love and determining to follow his ways. Choose kindness, honor, and integrity in everything you do today, remembering his audience is the one that matters most.

Active Remembrance

"You shall also teach them to your sons, speaking of them when you sit in your house, when you walk along the road, when you lie down, and when you get up."

DEUTERONOMY 11:19 NASB

We talk about the things that are important to us. Or at least, we should! If we spend all our time on things that don't matter, we will find our lives run by afterthoughts. However, if we choose to value the important things with our attention, time, and relationships, they will not go missed.

As we actively put God's Word and promises at the forefront of our lives, sharing them with others becomes natural. Talking about them, thinking about them, these things will happen more and more as we take God's instructions seriously. And his very Spirit is there to remind us of when we a nudge in the right direction.

Pick one promise of God to keep coming back to today. Write it down and put it in a place (or even multiple places) where you will see it throughout your day.

Start with Purpose

Very early in the morning, while it was still dark, Jesus got up, left the house and went off to a solitary place, where he prayed.

MARK 1:35 NIV

Jesus made time with the Father a priority in his life. He did not wait until his disciples were up to pray. He cultivated his own relationship with God in solitude. In the same way, we can privately encourage our own souls in devotion to God as we spend time in his presence and get to know him more. Our prayer lives are as unique as each of us, but we all have the same access to the Father through Christ.

How we begin our day can set the tone for how it plays out. We cannot always control what this looks like, but we can steal even just a few moments away by ourselves to set our hearts straight and give God our attention. Even if we are physically surrounded, our hearts can be in deep communion with the Spirit. Our reliance on God can greatly increase our hope and keep our eyes open to creative solutions as he shows us the ways of his wisdom.

Be intentional about taking even a few minutes to start your day in prayer today.

Invitation to Rest

"Come to Me, all you who labor and are heavy laden,
and I will give you rest."

MATTHEW 11:28 NKJV

When our bodies, minds, and hearts are spent, there is nothing more that we can do. We need to rest. This is not giving up! Rest is as essential to our progress as the work we do. In strength training, our bodies need rest to recover. In learning, our brains need breaks to process the information we take in. Rest is powerful, and it is an important part of our healing, our recovery, and our growth.

Take Jesus' invitation seriously today. Come to him with your burdens and lay them at his feet. He can handle the weight of them. There are times when you need to stop. You need to take breaks. You need to rest! This is how you were created, so don't resist it. If you do, you may find that you are pushed to a breaking point, and that is not what God wants for you. No, take his hand, as he leads you into rest.

Read through Psalm 23. This is a picture of God's tender care for you. Let yourself off the hook when you are tired. Honor your body, your mind, and your heart, and do what you so desperately need to do—REST.

May

Blessed be the God and Father of our Lord Jesus Christ. Because of his great mercy he has given us new birth into a living hope through the resurrection of Jesus Christ from the dead.

1 PETER 1:3 CSB

Keep Reaching

I know that I have not yet reached that goal, but there is one thing I always do. Forgetting the past and straining toward what is ahead, I keep trying to reach the goal and get the prize for which God called me through Christ to the life above.

PHILIPPIANS 3:13-14 NCV

Hope propels us and motivates us because it gives us something to look forward to. Hope is the possibility of what can be. It is a picture or goal of what we want to accomplish, or see come to reality. It offers us vision, clarity, and purpose. Knowing what our goals are, we can more easily align our choices to move us in that direction. It may require us to say no to things that take up too much room in our lives. It may require more defined boundaries. This is not a bad thing! When we know what we are reaching for, we also can see the things we need to let go of in the now to move toward it.

The work will sometimes feel like sacrifice. It will take intention and discipline. In short: some days the work will feel like work. That does not make it any less spiritual. Know what you are moving toward, and you can confidently make your plans for today.

What do you need to say no to today (or perhaps in this season) to make more room for movement toward your goal? What can you say yes to?

Blessing of God

Even if you happen to suffer for doing what is right, you will have the joyful experience of the blessing of God. And Don't be intimidated or terrified by those who would terrify you.

1 PETER 3:14 TPT

Doing the right thing can, in fact, be its own reward. We have no reason to question our conscience or our decisions. When we know that we have acted in loving kindness, doing what Christ himself would have done, then we have no reason to give into fear or regret.

Freedom from the fear of being found out is a by-product of living with integrity. When we have nothing to hide, we can live with our attention on what is right, what is true, what is lovely. Even when others ridicule our choices or try to make our lives harder for us because they disagree, even then we can know the blessing of choosing to do the right thing. Hope keeps our eyes clear and our hearts free from intimidation!

Does intimidation or fear of what others may think keep you from doing what you know to be right? Ask the Lord for courage to move toward hope with integrity, love, and perseverance.

Gracious Favor

She gleaned in the field until evening. Then she beat out what she had gleaned, and it was about an ephah of barley.

RUTH 2:17 ESV

Part of the reason that Ruth found favor with Boaz was the fact that she found ways to provide for her mother-in-law, Naomi, by going out to pick up leftover grain. When he saw her diligence in coming day after day, he instructed his farm workers to let her pick from whatever she found. In his good graces, she came home with an abundance of wheat, and it was through hard work partnered with favor from Boaz.

Boaz reflects God's gracious heart toward us. He blesses our work with favor, and we collect far more than we could have imagined at the start. This is an element of hope, too. As we move toward our hope with solutions and putting in the work we know to do, we find that when we are in the right place at the right time, God's generosity increases our fruitfulness.

Take courage and hope from the story of Ruth and Boaz and trust that when you put in the work, God will provide for you and bless you beyond what you can imagine.

Consistency Is Key

The plans of the diligent certainly lead to profit,
but anyone who is reckless certainly becomes poor.

PROVERBS 21:5 CSB

Don't overlook the power of consistency in your life. It is not the person who has the most unique idea that gets the most fruit in this life; it is the person who works at it, day in and day out. A brilliant idea without follow through is worthless, but consistent work at even the mundane, can bring about a great profit.

Hope helps us to be consistent. The desire to see the possibility become reality drives us to work at it in actionable ways. A hasty decision may feel like a good idea in the moment, but if we don't have foresight or consistency to back it up, it may just lead us into a reckless way of living. It is much better to follow a plan that brings about slow change than to hope for an overnight transformation without any effort on our part. The person who knows how to work diligently will always have options in their corner.

Be mindful and intentional about what you want to work toward this week, month, year (and maybe even beyond). Line up your schedule with the work it will take to get there and break it down into manageable chunks! Then, do the work, and keep on doing it.

Rebuilding in Hope

At last the wall was completed to half its height around the
entire city, for the people had worked with enthusiasm.

NEHEMIAH 4:6 NLT

Nehemiah 4 tells of the rebuilding of the wall of Jerusalem.
Though it was but a heap of rubble, Nehemiah and the Hebrew
nation worked with enthusiasm, and as they did, they saw
the fruit of their labor. Hope can be an act of defiance in the
face of those who don't believe that it is possible. For those
who take hold of it, the enthusiasm of seeing it come to life
motivates their hands to do the work!

Some hopes are our own, and some we must band together
to achieve. Nehemiah could not have rebuilt the wall on his
own, but with people who were enthusiastic about the work,
it was built to half its original height. This was enough to make
people take notice. Let's not ignore the power of uniting our
hopes with others and working to make each other's hopes a
reality!

Hope is most powerful in the face of uncertainty. Hope
motivates you to rebuild instead of despairing in what once
was. This echoes the heart of God, for he is restorer and
redeemer. What dream do you have the enthusiasm to put
toward rebuilding?

Undeterred

Every day, in the temple and from house to house, they did not stop teaching and preaching the good news of Jesus as the Christ.

ACTS 5:42 NASB

The apostles never stopped teaching and preaching the good news of Christ. Even when they faced persecution and suffered for it, they would not be deterred from their primary purpose. Christ had utterly transformed their lives and their hopes, and they would not stop sharing the good news of great hope with all who would listen.

Challenges are not enough to stop us when our hope is set on something much greater than the ease with which we move toward it. The grace of God empowers us in strength, joy, peace, and perseverance. If we do not know the reason why we are doing what we are doing, we may simply give up when it gets difficult. However, if we build our hope on the foundation of God's promises, we always have reason to persist.

Aside from your own personal hopes in life, be sure to live with the kingdom values of Christ as your sail and rudder. They will direct you and keep you going, for you can navigate the storms knowing that the shores of his kingdom are on the horizon!

Due Diligence

If it is to encourage, then give encouragement; if it is giving, then give generously; if it is to lead, do it diligently; if it is to show mercy, do it cheerfully.

ROMANS 12:8 NIV

It is a beautiful thing that we each have unique gifts. Not all of us are teachers, not all of us are leaders. But that does not mean that we are worth any less to God or to his kingdom. Our work, no matter what it is, matters. Our diligence to do what is ours to do is what propels us forward in life.

When we get caught up in comparison, we may lose sight of our own gifts. We must learn to let go of the trap of trying to be like others, and simply live out the lives we have with determination and diligence. We get to enjoy ourselves along the way, too! The more we learn who we are, the more comfortable we can become in delighting in who God created us to be. There truly is freedom in this way of life. Hope exists for each of us, though it may look different. We don't have to judge each other *or* be jealous of one another. We can simply live in the delight of our own lives and how God meets us there while honoring him with our surrender to his love.

Every time you find yourself either judging or comparing your life to another's, turn your attention to the blessings and gifts of your own person and life. Choose to delight in what is yours, and that delight will grow!

Stay in the Present

"Do not worry about tomorrow,
for tomorrow will worry about its own things.
Sufficient for the day is its own trouble."

MATTHEW 6:34 NKJV

If we remain focused on the possible troubles of tomorrow, we miss out on the opportunity to deal with what comes our way today. Preoccupation with the future isn't healthy or helpful. It can cause us to worry, and perhaps even to give up. Hope thrives in the soil of grace, and we need grace for each moment. We can't reach into the future and receive grace. We receive it as often as we require it, but only in the present.

When we give God our worries, as Jesus tells us to do, we can focus on each challenge as it comes our way. His wisdom is our ready help. His peace gives us clarity. His love allows us to face reality head on with hope. Hope gives us eyes to see how we can take steps forward in God's ways. Worry only hampers us. We truly can trust God, bringing him our worries whenever they pop up, and leave them with him. He is always ready to help us when we need it!

When you are tempted to jump ahead into worry about unknowns you have no control over, take them to God in prayer. Ask for the wisdom and grace to deal with the challenges of today, instead.

Rejoice in Hope

Be joyful because you have hope.
Be patient when trouble comes, and pray at all times.

ROMANS 12:12 NCV

Having hope is reason to rejoice. When we believe in the possibility of goodness, we choose the path of faith that is paved with God's faithfulness. We trust him because he is trustworthy. We follow him because he is a good leader. He never leaves us or forsakes us. We can rely on him in the good times and in the terrible times. And when those terrible times come, we can practice patience, knowing that they are not the end of our story or the story of God's loyal love.

Prayer can be a lifeline in such times. While it is always a good time to connect to the Lord, reaching out to him when our souls are struggling is especially important. He doesn't ever require us to walk the path of our lives alone. He is always near, and he is quick to comfort. Let's rely on his presence as much as we do the air we breathe. Even when we don't think about it, he is our sustenance and strength!

Always pray, through every circumstance of your day. Give God your joy and your heartache. Lean in, beloved, and keep leaning.

Just Ask

"Until now you've not been bold enough to ask the Father
for a single thing in my name, but now you can ask, and
keep on asking him! And you can be sure that you'll receive
what you ask for, and your joy will have no limits!"

JOHN 16:24 TPT

Ask and keep on asking. These are the encouraging words
of Christ. We don't have to ask and then avoid broaching
the same question again. We can ask as many times as is
necessary for our hearts to believe. We can bring God our
questions and doubt, and he won't be offended. He really is
that good!

When we foster cultures of hope, we create communities that
both support and uplift each other. Let's not overlook the
power of prayer in these actions. As we make our requests to
God, we can do them alone *and* with others. Then, one answer
to prayer is an encouragement to all! Let's cultivate our hope
in the people we choose to build our lives with and ask God
together for the breakthrough that we long for!

*Ask at least one person if there is something that you can
pray for about them or their lives, and when they tell you, do
it! As you remember them later, pray for them again, thanking
the Father for his goodness toward them.*

Source of Wisdom

"Call to me and I will answer you, and will tell you great
and hidden things that you have not known."

JEREMIAH 33:3 ESV

The wisdom of God gives us clarity. When we don't know
what to do, we should ask God, who gives freely to all who
ask. As James 1:5 says, "If any of you lacks wisdom, let him
ask God, who gives generously to all without reproach, and it
will be given him." God's ways are better than our own, for his
wisdom takes everything into account, all that we can see and
so much more that we cannot.

When we find ourselves in need, it is to our honor when
we reach out for help. None of us is perfect in wisdom.
We shouldn't pretend to be! What we don't know is an
opportunity to learn and grow from others. Humility keeps us
open and learning, and that is a beautiful thing.

*Admitting that you do not know something is an open door
to receiving wisdom. Ask the Lord for the right connections,
as well as for revelation of his kingdom ways. Don't resist the
perspectives of others but weigh their advice with wisdom
and discernment.*

Take Your Sabbath

A Sabbath rest remains for God's people. For the person who has entered his rest has rested from his own works, just as God did from his.

HEBREWS 4:9-10 CSB

God took a break from work on the seventh day, and the principle of Sabbath remains as an important way for us to refresh our bodies, minds, and souls. Our society isn't great at taking a full day of rest. Productivity guilt plagues many of us, but this is not from God. It's not what we were intended to live with. Rest is holy! It is necessary, and the example God set for us.

If we don't prioritize or protect our time, we may find that we work ourselves ragged. Still others of us may physically be choosing rest but battle our minds telling us we should be doing differently. True rest is not only physical, but also mental, spiritual, and emotional, as well. Rest can look different for each of us, but we must not resist the things that rejuvenate and refresh us: body, soul, and spirit.

Your Sabbath doesn't have to be Saturday or Sunday, it can be whatever day works best for your schedule. Be sure to schedule a rest day and protect it. Plan it out for the next month, at least, and take your rest as seriously as you do your work.

Wisdom Produces Patience

People with understanding control their anger;
a hot temper shows great foolishness.

PROVERBS 14:29 NLT

The ability to control our reactions is a powerful indicator of wisdom. Anger itself is not a bad thing. It cues us to a boundary that may have been crossed or a need ignored. It can be a reaction to something unjust. However, when we fly off the handle often and without warning, it signifies that we have little self-restraint.

Self-regulation has been shown in research to be linked to higher levels of hope. Hope, as we already know, is not just a theory, but the ability to make goals and achieve them. When we practice patience and self-control, we can give ourselves the space and clarity to choose what is best. Every hope has its own path to get there, but the act of self-regulation is paramount no matter the steps taken.

When you feel yourself getting activated (either in frustration, anger, or another strong emotion), take a moment to breathe and step away, if need be. Lead with curiosity and a desire to understand rather than simply reacting.

Just a Breath

A thousand years in Your sight
Are like yesterday when it passes by,
Or like a watch in the night.

PSALM 90:4 NASB

Time can feel like such a weird thing. One moment you are young, and the next you are approaching middle age. Though time seems to draw out in our youth, it truly does feel as if it is flying by the older we get. Our lives are short, but the present moment in each and every day is where we build, brick by brick. Being sure to be intentional with our values, our goals, and our relationships will help us to use the time we have wisely.

God is so gracious. He knows what we need, and he provides for us. As we partner with his purposes, he blesses the work of our hands. Perspective can help us remember the important things of life and what we want to put our efforts toward. When we realize how fleeting life can be, our purpose and desires are clarified. We may not know the number of our days, but we can certainly live each one with intention, wisdom, and presence.

Not every day of your life will feel significant. It is important to know the power of simplicity in your life. What are your hopes about your life when it is all said and done? Refine your expectations and your tasks around those things.

Searched and Known

You have searched me, LORD, and you know me.
You know when I sit and when I rise;
you perceive my thoughts from afar.

PSALM 139:1-2 NIV

Knowing that God can search our hearts should not cause us to fear. Hopefully, it brings a sense of relief. He sees the good, the bad, and everything in between. He has no misconceived notions about who you are. The even greater news than this is the fact that he loves you completely. His kindness leads us to repentance. His mercy covers our failures and flaws. He accepts us as his children. We have only to humble ourselves before him and yield to his beautiful ways.

There is nothing you could do to make God rescind his love. You have the freedom to choose how you will live, and if you trust God's heart, you will follow his love wherever it leads. You don't have to be afraid. You don't have to hide your questions, either. Come as you are to the one who knows you through and through.

Read through the whole of Psalm 139. Ask the Lord for greater revelation of his affection for you and let that motivate you today.

Belief in Action

Without faith it is impossible to please Him, for he who comes to God must believe that He is, and that He is a rewarder of those who diligently seek Him.

HEBREWS 11:6 NKJV

Belief is the seed, and desire keeps us attentive to tending to it. The chapter goes on to describe the power of faith through the lives of men and women who had gone before. Faith is a motivator and strong foundation. It is closely linked to hope; together, they produce lives filled with purpose.

Faith and hope both require trust and persistence in something that is not fully formed (or seen) yet. The revelation of God gives us glimpses to harness our faith to. Hope gives us something to work toward. They require both trust and action, and as we do both, our ability to believe and to move ahead in hope increases.

Identify a challenge to your faith or hope today and determine what you can do to take an actionable step toward it today.

Beautiful in Its Time

God has given them a desire to know the future. He does everything just right and on time, but people can never completely understand what he is doing.

ECCLESIASTES 3:11 NCV

It is so important to keep our perspectives in check. Though we may know some things, there are things at work, both in the world and in our lives, which we cannot fully understand. This is not a failure on our part. This is part of being human. There is one, however, who does everything right and on time. We can trust him to weave mercy through the details of our stories, through every season of our lives.

If you are living, God has not given up on you. He has not removed his mercy from your life. Let your desire move you toward greater reliance on his faithfulness. Trust that even when you cannot see a solution for a problem, that does not mean that God isn't working to bring it together for your good. He makes all things beautiful in their time!

When you cannot understand how something will turn out, turn your heart in prayer to God. Ask for his present peace to wash over you that you may trust him more.

Choose Wisdom

Whoever is wise, let him understand these things;
whoever is discerning, let him know them
for the ways of the LORD are right,
and the upright walk in them,
but transgressors stumble in them.

HOSEA 14:9 ESV

If we want to walk in the way of God's wisdom, we must be willing to recognize and trust the one who created us. It is wisdom that recognizes where our fruitfulness stems from, not from the power of our own abilities, but from God himself.

The ways of the Lord are right. We don't have to understand everything about God to choose to walk in his ways. However, the Lord will continue to reveal himself to us as we follow his lead. His love paves a path that leads to joy, peace, patience, kindness, gentleness, self-control; all the fruits of the Spirit are there! They strengthen and help us along the way and give us clues as to when we may be drifting from God's ways into the ways of this world (which are selfish, cruel, and divisive). Choose wisdom by choosing the path of Christ today and every day.

Get clear about what God's ways look like. Especially learn from the life and ministry of Christ, who showed us the way to the Father.

Guard Your Affections

Above all, guard the affections of your heart
for they affect all that you are.
Pay attention to the welfare of your innermost being
for from there flows the wellspring of life.

PROVERBS 4:23 TPT

Our hearts direct the course of our lives. From the desires
we cultivate, we find the motivation to move toward them.
It is important, then, that we realize the driving force of our
choices! Our innermost beings need as much care as our
bodies do. When we take the time to tend to them, we are
more apt to recognize when something is off.

Physical well checks are an expected part of our development.
We know that going to the doctor preemptively is a good
way to stay healthy and catch things early. If we are not doing
the same kind of intentional check-ins with our emotional
wellbeing, we may miss out on something important that
needs our attention. The affections of our hearts guide us
into all sorts of decisions, so keeping track of the root of our
motivations is important to the trajectory of our lives.

*Having tools to check in with our hearts, thoughts, and
emotions can be as powerful as our personal check-ins. Talk
to a mentor, counselor, or follow journal prompts to check in
on the state of your heart today.*

Living Word

The word of God is living and effective and sharper
than any double-edged sword, penetrating as far as the
separation of soul and spirit, joints and marrow. It is able to
judge the thoughts and intentions of the heart.

HEBREWS 4:12 CSB

Perhaps you have experienced the piercing of God's Word in
your own heart and life. If you have, you know that it is exact
and true. It is clear and powerful. It can be the difference
between apathy and knowing exactly what needs to be
done. The wisdom of God is not without the power of God's
love. The living Word of God breathes life into our bones,
illuminating what once was hidden in the shadows.

Hope brings clarity, as well. One revelation from God can act
as a clear motivator. It can help us align the rest of our lives
toward that end. God doesn't give us so many directives that
we don't know where to start. Following him is not always
easy, but it certainly is simple. God has a right-now word to
give you the focus you need. Ask him for it!

*The living Word of God is always powerful and effective. Pray
and ask God for the vision you need, both for today and for
this season you are in.*

Mark Out the Path

Mark out a straight path for your feet;
stay on the safe path.

PROVERBS 4:26 NLT

Hope is a way of thinking. It is a perspective that sees beyond our circumstances and to the goals we have for the future. To make a path, we must first know where we want to end up. We may not always know which way the path will wind along the way, but we can take the next step toward the hope as we keep it before us.

Active hope keeps us motivated. Movement gets us closer to the goal. Perspective and aligning our steps in faith keep us pressing on toward the end. Even when we come up against obstacles in our path, hope sees possibility. It can forge a creative way around it. And even when we cannot, God shows us a way out. He is always faithful to come through when we call on him for help!

Take some time today to evaluate your goals and consider how your life is leading to them. If there is a gap, consider what next steps would get you closer and incorporate them in the coming days and weeks. Keep marking that path!

Release It

"Do not be worried about your life, as to what you will eat or what you will drink; nor for your body, as to what you will put on. Is life not more than food, and the body more than clothing?"

MATTHEW 6:25 NASB

We can only do what we can do. Does that sound familiar, or perhaps a bit trite? The fact remains, we cannot control what we will come up against in this life, but we can approach every challenge with openness and trust. God will not let us starve. He is a good provider. God provided manna in the desert for his people: bread sent straight from heaven every single day! There is grace to find our provision in him, too.

Worry seems a normal state for many of us, though that is not what Christ wants for us. He wants us to trust our good Father for all that we need. Worry can be a waste of energy because it doesn't change a thing. Let's do what we can do and leave the rest with God. He will take care of us!

When worry starts to creep into your heart or mind today, consider if there is anything you can do about it at this moment. If the answer is no, release it to God. He is faithful and trustworthy.

Higher Power

To him who is able to do immeasurably more than all we ask or imagine, according to his power that is at work within us, to him be glory in the church and in Christ Jesus throughout all generations, for ever and ever! Amen.

EPHESIANS 3:20-21 NIV

We can only do so much with the time and resources we have been given. Graciously, God can do far more than we could ever ask or imagine. His solutions and power know no end. What a relief! When we are stumped, he is not. When we come up against a dead end, he shows us the way around, and sometimes, by faith, he asks us to follow him through what we cannot see or understand.

Hope does far more for our hearts than motivate us. It keeps us open to possibility. When challenges arise, hope keeps us resilient and creative. It keeps us trusting and optimistic that there is another way, even if we don't know what that way is yet. When we put our trust in God, we tether our hope to his infinite power, which is rooted in his relentless lovingkindness.

Make a slight shift in your prayers today. Instead of pleading with God to change your circumstances, put those circumstances up to the possibilities of what God can do. The result may be the same, but the expectation of your heart may feel lighter.

A Gentle Approach

Let your gentleness be known to all men.
The Lord is at hand.

PHILIPPIANS 4:5 NKJV

One of the fruits of the Spirit is gentleness. An attribute of gentleness is humility, not thinking of ourselves as better than others. Gentleness comes from a place of understanding. Rather than seeking to put someone in their place, gentleness fosters a kind approach. God himself takes this approach to us! Romans 2:4 tells us that it is the kindness of God that leads us to repentance. Knowing this is how God works, if we want to be more like him, then we also will choose to lead with kindness.

Proverbs 15:1 reminds us, "a soft answer turns away wrath, But a harsh word stirs up anger." We can foster hope in our relationships by being kind, compassionate, and open to change. Hope sees the possibility for a different outcome, and it adjusts to make the end possible. If we want transformation in our relationships, gentleness is a powerful way to practice hopeful action.

Be intentional about approaching others (conversations, interactions, etc.) with gentleness.

Sweet as Honey

Pleasant words are like a honeycomb,
making people happy and healthy.

PROVERBS 16:24 NCV

Lifegiving words are those that bring encouragement and kindness. They promote peace and encourage understanding. They are laced with love. Pleasant words can speak the truth in love, and this not seeking to shame anyone, but sharing from a heart that wants what is best for everyone.

We know the difference between words meant to guilt us and words meant to encourage us. In our souls, we feel the lightness and healing of love at work. It is a worthwhile endeavor to encourage others. It doesn't come from superficial compliments, but from others feeling seen, known, loved, and accepted.

Choose to speak kind, true words to those in your sphere today. Be intentional about it. Send texts to those who are far away.

Selfless Love

If anyone sees a fellow believer in need and has the means to help him, yet shows no pity and closes his heart against him, how is it even possible that God's love lives in him?

1 JOHN 3:17 TPT

Love is not just an emotion; it is a choice. It is a compelling motivator for action. Love without evidence is not love at all. It remains a vague idea or nice notion if it is not put into action. If we want to love like Christ calls us to, then a good place to start is by choosing it, even when it feels like a sacrifice.

Consider the parable of the Good Samaritan in Luke 10. When a religious scholar questioned Jesus about the letter of the law (loving God and loving one's neighbor) he pressed to know who is considered his neighbor. It seems he was looking for a reason to love some and not others, but Jesus' parable exemplified that a true neighbor is one who demonstrates kindness and mercy, regardless of the identity of the person in need. When we look for reasons to excuse our lack of love, we miss the point entirely. Love sacrifices, and it shows kindness and mercy to all who need it.

Go out of your way to perform small acts of kindness to others today, no matter who they are.

Impossible to Forget

"Can a woman forget her nursing child, that she should have no compassion on the son of her womb? Even these may forget, yet I will not forget you. Behold, I have engraved you on the palms of my hands; your walls are continually before me."

ISAIAH 49:15-16 ESV

It is not likely that a mother would forget her nursing child. The bond between mother and child keeps her body, as well as her heart and mind, tied to the child's needs. Even if biology were to fail, however, God says that he would never forget his children. Though the improbable happens in this world, the impossible truth is that God sees, knows, and loves us with a kindness we can't even imagine. He is attentive to the needs of his children. He cannot and will not forget us.

Relationships can strengthen our hope. How much more will a deep relationship with our Creator, then, strengthen the hope we have? His care of us is a balm of comfort and a dash of courage. His love strengthens us from the inside out. We are never alone, not even on our hardest days.

Open your heart to the Lord and ask him to show you what he thinks of you. Take hope in his Word and in his knowledge of your life. He loves you, so let him love you to life!

Real and Ready Help

We do not have a high priest who is unable to sympathize with our weaknesses, but one who has been tempted in every way as we are, yet without sin.

HEBREWS 4:15 CSB

Have you ever felt like you are alone in your struggle, like no one else could possibly understand what you are going through? Graciously, you are not alone even when you feel like it. Today's verse reminds us that Jesus was tempted in every way, but he did not sin. He is acquainted with sorrow and suffering. He knows what it is like to hunger, to thirst, to grieve, and to long. He knows, he truly knows, what you are going through.

Weakness is not a sin. Remember this well. Weakness is evidence of your humanity. You will grow tired and weary, and you will need to rest. Christ offers grace and strength to empower you. He offers solidarity so that you feel seen. The particulars of your struggle may look different than his but make no mistake about it: there is hope in him.

When you struggle to hope, remember that God makes all things new, and he offers direction in the mercy of his wisdom. Lean into the presence of God and depend on him even when you feel isolated from others.

Uplifted

Humble yourselves before the Lord,
and he will lift you up in honor.

JAMES 4:10 NLT

Although pride often goes before a fall, the opposite also rings true. Humility leads to honor. It is always a good idea to stay humble in our hearts, both before God and before others. We can be humble and confident, for humility is the ability to redirect and admit when we are wrong and change for the better. An openness to keep learning throughout our lives leads to increased understanding. Honor comes to those who are willing and choose to grow, rather than stay rigid in their views.

When we humble ourselves before God, he lifts us up in his power and love. Instead of judging others, we simply obey his law of love. He is the only one wise enough to judge hearts, so let's leave that to him. What we take up is the control over our own hearts and lives! We are responsible for our own attitudes and thoughts. Let's give up the energy of trying to manage others when we need to focus on our own hearts.

Put your energy toward your own heart and life by humbling yourself before God. When you jump to judgment, redirect your heart in prayer and ask for the grace to see the state of your own heart and what you can do to change.

No Matter What

"The mountains may be removed and the hills may shake,
But My favor will not be removed from you,
Nor will My covenant of peace be shaken,"
Says the Lord who has compassion on you.

ISAIAH 54:10 NASB

Nothing can separate us from the love of God. Paul confirmed this in Romans 8:38-39: "For I am convinced that neither death, nor life, nor angels, nor principalities, nor things present, nor things to come, nor powers, nor height, nor depth, nor any other created thing will be able to separate us." Even if the mountains were thrown into the sea, the love of God would remain.

Where there is love, there is hope. Hope for redemption, hope for solutions, hope for a new day. Whatever you are going through, you cannot escape the extravagant love of God. What courage there is in realizing there is nothing in heaven or on earth, nothing that you could ever do or not do, to separate you from the merciful power of God's love through Christ!

When you feel overwhelmed today, take a moment to lean into the presence of God. Let love lead you to hope!

Every Merciful Moment

"If my people, who are called by my name, will humble themselves and pray and seek my face and turn from their wicked ways, then I will hear from heaven, and I will forgive their sin and will heal their land."

2 Chronicles 7:14 NIV

There isn't a moment that we are without the mercy of God. There is also the opportunity to course-correct at any time. We can humble ourselves before the Lord whenever we choose to. We can ask for forgiveness and help in every circumstance. We are never too far gone.

God never turns away from those who call on him for help. Isaiah 59:1 says, "Surely the arm of the Lord is not too short to save, nor his ear too dull to hear." When we humble ourselves before God, we allow him to meet us in the reality of where we are. We don't deny his help or ignore his teachings. There is so much hope in the realization that God's heart is ready to forgive and pour out mercy whenever we turn to him.

Is there an area where you have been resisting God? Choose humility before him today and allow him to speak to your situation in mercy.

June

With your minds ready for action,
be sober-minded and set your hope
completely on the grace to be brought
to you at the revelation of Jesus Christ.

1 PETER 1:13 CSB

Pathways of Life

You will show me the path of life
In Your presence is fullness of joy;
At Your right hand are pleasures forevermore.

PSALM 16:11 NKJV

The path that Jesus leads us down is full of life, and abundant life, at that. With God as our leader, we have everything we need. He meets our needs from the abundant resources of his being and kingdom.

If we have not experienced joy in the presence of God, then we need a glimpse of his glorious goodness! Let us ask for our eyes to be opened to the faithfulness of God at work in our lives. As long as we've been living, God's hand of mercy has been present. What joy there is in the knowledge of God's nearness. With hearts of expectancy, hope propels us in joy in the inescapable kindness of God with us.

The more you get to know God, the more pleasure you experience in the revelation of who he is. He is more powerful, more loving, so much better in every way, than you give him credit for. Spend time in his presence and ask him to show you where he has been faithful in kindness toward you. Celebrate in joy every revelation he gives.

Arising in Comfort

The LORD wants to show his mercy to you.
He wants to rise and comfort you.
The LORD is a fair God, and everyone who waits for his help
will be happy.

ISAIAH 30:18 NCV

The desire of God is not to destroy, but to give life. He is full of mercy, and this mercy offers the promise of redemption, renewal, and a fresh new start! God does not arise in anger toward you when you call out to him. He is full of comfort and compassion.

The more we experience the comfort of God's love, the more readily we can extend compassion and comfort to those around us. When our friends are suffering, we don't have to fix it. We can simply draw near to them with love and offer the comfort of our presence. Sometimes, that is what makes all the difference. Showing up is a powerful action. We don't have to have answers or solutions to extend compassion and care to others.

Instead of keeping your distance from a friend or loved one who is suffering, spend time with them. Offer comfort, whether through a listening ear, keeping them company, doing the dishes, or bringing them food. Presence speaks louder than a few words ever could.

Fullness of Joy

"My purpose for telling you these things is
so that the joy that I experience will fill your hearts
with overflowing gladness!"

JOHN 15:11 TPT

How do we experience overflowing gladness in Christ? We do it by letting the love of Christ nourish our hearts, and by keeping his commands. As we obey him, we choose to live in his love. Jesus told his disciples that he lived continually nourished and empowered by the love of the Father, and that was his hope for each of them.

There is so much joy when we know the extent of God's love for us. It fills us up, rooting our identities in who he says we are. It nourishes and empowers us to love others. It helps us to lean in and to also to let go. Overflowing joy is a promise he gives to all those who learn to live in the power of his love!

The act of continually living nourished and empowered in God's love (John 15:10) leads to gladness. Make spending time in prayer and fellowship with the Spirit a priority every day.

Light in the Tunnel

After you have suffered a little while, the God of all grace, who has called you to his eternal glory in Christ, will himself restore, confirm, strengthen, and establish you.

1 PETER 5:10 ESV

When we walk through valleys of sorrow and suffering, it can feel as if we will never cross through to the other side. Today's verse is a reminder that no suffering is forever. All our troubles are temporary, but the promised glory of God is eternal. We may struggle for a time, but it is nothing compared to the glory that awaits us.

The presence of God with us in our troubles is a light in the darkness. The encouragement of his Word as he speaks lights a flame of hope that reminds us that the end has not come. There is a bright new day that will dawn. We have only to trust and to keep leaning on the one who leads us, still. Even when his voice is a whisper, that just means that he's close enough that we might hear it. He will not let us go. His presence lights up our dark nights, and the hope of his coming is even brighter than we have yet seen.

Hope helps you to keep going. Whatever you're working toward today, remember it so that when challenges arise, you can still choose to press on.

Still Working

I am sure of this, that he who started a good work in you
will carry it on to completion until the day of Christ Jesus.

PHILIPPIANS 1:6 CSB

The good that is in your life is a gift from God. It is evidence of
God's mercy at work within you. He who started this work will
not give up and won't let go. He will carry it on to completion.

Our partnership with God is important; there is work for
us to do, in both the choices we make and the way we act
toward others. However, we shouldn't be discouraged when
the season changes and, with it, the terrain of our lives. We
cannot expect a harvest of fruitfulness in the winter. Let's not
lose hope when the work of God in our lives seems dormant.
Perhaps it has just gone beneath the surface for a time.
Though we cannot see it, our roots may still be growing deep
and the connections of our heart to the Father, stronger.

*If it is hard to pinpoint forward motion in your life, ask the
Lord what he is doing in this area. Wait on his wisdom, and
trust him to continue the work, even if it is hard to see.*

Every Step of the Way

"The LORD your God is going with you!
He will fight for you against your enemies,
and he will give you victory!"

DEUTERONOMY 20:4 NLT

There are times when it will feel as though you are forging a new path. Even when no one else goes with you, the Lord does. Trust him to guide you in the wilderness seasons, for he is faithful and true. He is a good shepherd and a reliable leader. He will fight for you when no one else comes to your aid. He really is that good!

When you trust that your victory belongs to the Lord, the pressure to perform perfectly lifts. It is good to prepare, but you don't have to wait for a complete plan to take the first step toward your desired end. Take the step, for your God goes with you every step of the way!

In areas where you have been hesitating to move ahead, take some time to consider the reason. If it is simply fear, know that God will not leave you. Let his presence be your courage. However, if there are valid reasons for your hesitation, ask God to redirect you toward the hope that is right for you to move toward in. In any case, trust him!

Taste and See

Taste and see that the Lord is good;
How blessed is the man who takes refuge in Him!

PSALM 34:8 NASB

A life without challenges doesn't afford many opportunities for growth. The goodness of God is not dependent on ease or the lack of suffering. God is as good in our trials as he is in our victories. In fact, the challenges help us grow—in hope, in love, in persistence, in joy—the list goes on!

If we want to grow in hope, we must embrace the challenges that come our way. Every trouble is an opportunity to grow in the grace of God as it meets us in every moment. Then, we will taste and see that the Lord is good, even as we take refuge in him!

Approach every challenge or hiccup today as an opportunity to experience the goodness of God in a new way.

It Is Covered

Above all, love each other deeply,
because love covers over a multitude of sins.

1 PETER 4:8 NIV

With love as our covering, we know that there is no better, wiser, godlier choice than to move in loving kindness toward each other. Forgiveness is an act of love, and so is trying to be better! Letting go of our offenses is important and liberating, and so is being kind for no other reason than it is our choice to do so.

We cannot escape the importance of love. If we take the Word of God seriously, there is no way around it. Love is the source from which all other life grows. If we want to walk in the liberty of Christ, we must choose to walk in his love. We fill up in the mercy of God, and we give it away. There is no need to keep it to ourselves; in fact, we should try to outdo one another in love. As we do, this kindness covers a multitude of wrongs.

Consider how apt you are to forgive someone who chooses humility, kindness, and the willingness to change. These are each an outgrowth of love. Do unto others as you would have them do to you.

The Law of Love

> "A new commandment I give to you, that you love one another; as I have loved you, that you also love one another. By this all will know that you are My disciples, if you have love for one another."
>
> JOHN 13:34-35 NKJV

There is perhaps no greater command than this. Loving one another is the power of God at work in our lives. The love of God is meant to be the source of all that we do, fueling our hope, joy, and peace. Love is not isolated, and it's not meant to keep to ourselves. We don't fill up simply to hoard it all. We are filled to pour out. With the same measure we've been given, we can offer to others.

If we take the Word of Christ seriously, we cannot ignore this command to love one another. This, Jesus says, is how the world will know that we are his. If we want others to know that we belong to Jesus, then we can't get around the law of his love. We show that we have the love of Christ in us when we love others. And love doesn't give up easily; it is not easily offended. It is not fickle. It is stronger than hatred and dividing lines drawn in the world. Love covers all!

Choose love in your interactions and choices. When you feel yourself tempted to excuse why you don't have to be loving, let that be your cue that love is exactly what is called for!

Protection and Strength

God is our protection and our strength.
He always helps in times of trouble.
So we will not be afraid even if the earth shakes,
or the mountains fall into the sea,
even if the oceans roar and foam,
or the mountains shake at the raging sea.

PSALM 46:1-3 NCV

If God remains the hope of our hearts, he is our confidence. Even when the earth shakes, our hope will not be shaken. Even if the mountains fall into the sea, we will not forget the one who promises to help us in times of trouble. He is there as our protection and strength through every possible challenge!

When we need courage, it can be incredibly helpful to remember the faithfulness of God in what we've already gone through. How has he led us through the trials of life so far? How has he delivered those who have gone before us? The testimony of God's faithfulness can be enough to bolster our faith and hope in the one who still conquers today.

Read through or listen to a testimony of God's faithfulness, whether from someone you know or don't know. Take heart and share your own testimonies of his goodness when given the chance.

Resist Judgment

As part of God's family, never speak against another family member, for when you slander a brother or sister you violate God's law of love. And your duty is not to make yourself a judge of the law of love by saying that it doesn't apply to you, but your duty is to obey it!

JAMES 4:11 TPT

Too many of us have taken God's Word and used it to judge others. This is in direct contrast to the teachings of Christ, who summed up the whole of the Law by saying that we are to love God and love others. The law of love applies to us all. As James put it: "your duty is to obey it."

What would it really look like to put the law of love into practice in your life? Every excuse to treat others with anything but kindness would go out the window. Judgment, hatred, and an unwillingness to listen to other perspectives would have to bow under the command of clothing yourself in compassion. Where there is love, there is hope for a brighter day, for unity, and for actionable change.

Consider how often you jump to judgment rather than trying to understand others in love. Commit this verse to memory and bring it to mind throughout your day.

Wait in Hope

For God alone, O my soul, wait in silence,
for my hope is from him.
Trust in him at all times, O people;
pour out your heart before him;
God is a refuge for us. Selah

PSALM 62:5, 8 ESV

Sometimes the thing that our hearts need most is to wait in silence. We need space in our day to quiet our souls and let God meet us in the stillness. If we need strength, joy, hope, peace—any of it—slowing down and making space for the expansive goodness of God's presence is always a good idea.

We could go from dawn to dusk without ever tuning into silence. There are endless options of feeding our ears and minds through media, music, and the like. But our brains need silence to decompress. We need the space of doing nothing to reset. Waiting can be an incredible practice in directing our hearts in hope. Let's take the opportunities we have this day to allow for silence, space, and the promise of God in it.

Instead of having something playing in the background throughout your day, be purposeful in adding silence to your day. Take a few minutes, undistracted, and just be. Invite God into that space and wait for him.

Faith's Momentum

Faith is the reality of what is hoped for,
the proof of what is not seen.

HEBREWS 11:1 CSB

Faith connects us to the hope we have; it moves us toward the possibility with practical steps that make it a reality. If we believe that something is possible, we act accordingly. If, however, we don't believe that something is possible, we won't do anything about it.

Faith and hope are both connected to things that we do not yet see. Even so, they are needed to give our present moment purpose and clarity. If we do not know what we are working toward in life, what our hopes are for the future, we don't know what we should say yes to and what we should say no to. Faith gives us clarity to align our choices with our hopes. As we step forward, we will find the path lit up before us, even if it is just one step at a time. We will see what is around us to engage with and work out as we take each step.

Your hopes are only as good as your faith in their possibility. Is there a hope that you have remained stagnant in but want to make movement in? Believe that it is possible, for with God all things are, and do what you can today to take an actionable step toward it.

Every Reason to Hope

That's why I take pleasure in my weaknesses, and in the insults, hardships, persecutions, and troubles that I suffer for Christ. For when I am weak, then I am strong.

2 CORINTHIANS 12:10 NLT

People with high levels of hope tend to be more resilient to hardship. They can see beyond the challenges into the positive outcomes that remain on the other side of them. Resilience is a factor in success because the fact is that no life, no path, no job—nothing—is without its challenges. If we give up at the first sign of trouble simply because it is hard, we rob ourselves of the satisfaction that perseverance can bring.

We may find that challenges make our priorities clear. If it truly isn't worth it to us, then maybe giving up is the right thing. We cannot do everything we want to do at the same time; we don't have that kind of capacity. But we can do a few things well. As we get clear about what our hopes are for this season of life, we can much more readily endure the challenges with clear-eyed vision.

In your weakness, the Spirit of God strengthens you. You rely on his grace. Write down two or three hopes you have for this specific season of your life and prioritize your days and weeks accordingly.

Eyes Fixed

I have set the LORD continually before me;
Because He is at my right hand, I will not be shaken.

PSALM 16:8 NASB

When our vision is clear, we can more readily adjust our steps to reach it. The more nebulous the vision, the greater chance there is that we will struggle to find our footing. God is as present in the details as he is in the big picture; we can't forget that. He cares as much about our hearts as he does the trajectory of our lives, in fact, much more so. Even if our vision is simply to love God well, it is enough to trickle down into the choices we make daily.

Philippians 4:6 encourages us not to be pulled in different directions. If we have competing hopes, this may just be what happens. We can have hopes that differ from each other, but if they require completely different directions in our lives, we will feel the tension of them. Instead of being pulled apart by them, let's submit them to the Lord and allow him to light up the shadows of confusion we may feel.

Pray and ask God for help and clarity around your hopes and around your efforts and time. He is infinitely wise. Seek him, and everything else will fall into its place.

Faithful Fulfillment

"No word from God will ever fail."

LUKE 1:37 NIV

Even when we mess up and it feels as if there is no hope of recovery, the Lord in his infinite power and mercy, never fails. He is always ready to restore the repentant heart. He sows mercy into our story, weaving together what didn't seem to possibly connect. Though we fail a thousand times, God remains faithful through it all. He cannot remove his loyal love, and he will never neglect to help those who call on him.

When our hopes don't happen on our timeline, or there are dreams that break our hearts as they fall apart before our very eyes, it can be incredibly disheartening. It is here, in these places, where we can press into the comfort of God. Even when our hearts are breaking, God's faithfulness remains constant and true. He can do far more than we could ask or imagine, so let's not run away from his love, for it will revive our hearts if we let it.

It is so important to remember that when your expectations are not met, that doesn't mean that God has failed. He is doing more in the details than you can see on the surface. Let go of the need to control the outcome and trust his faithfulness to you!

Work to Do

"Arise, for this matter is your responsibility.
We also are with you. Be of good courage, and do it."

Ezra 10:4 NKJV

If we wait around for someone else to do the work that is plainly ours to do, we will waste time doing just that. We cannot pawn off our responsibilities to others and expect that our hopes will magically appear. There are things that you may be able to ask for help with, but that does not eliminate the work that remains yours to do. There are some responsibilities that belong to you and no one else.

Hope combines belief with desire. If we truly want to see that hope become a reality, we will take the steps necessary and do the work that is our responsibility to do. This doesn't mean we don't need encouragement sometimes. Today's verse demonstrates this well: a reminder of responsibility, but also the encouragement of support and to press on and do the work. This may seem like a bit of a kick in the pants, but the truth is that we need that sometimes! The support of friends can make all the difference. Even just knowing that they are cheering us on, and they want to see us succeed can give us the courage we need.

Is there a responsibility you have been avoiding? Do the work and lean into the support of your community if you need encouragement. But at the end of the day, do the work!

Upside-down Kingdom

He chose what the world thinks is unimportant and what the world looks down on and thinks is nothing in order to destroy what the world thinks is important. God did this so that no one can brag in his presence.

1 CORINTHIANS 1:28-29 NCV

If any of us has reason to think we can brag before God, we better prepare ourselves for a humbling. If we want to be great in the kingdom of heaven, the most important step toward that is to remain humble before God and others.

God doesn't look down upon the things we may disparage. He doesn't ignore the poor or prefer the powerful. He doesn't need the highly skilled to move in mighty ways. He can take the most humble, ordinary people and do great things through their yielded lives. He does this so that we remember that God's ways are higher than our own, and he doesn't judge people based on how the world and its systems do.

See if you can catch pride when it pops up in your reactions to the people and places around you. Hope sees possibilities, and it knows that nothing is impossible with God.

Moved by the Spirit

The mature children of God are those who are moved by the impulses of the Holy Spirit.

ROMANS 8:14 TPT

Romans 15:13 says that God is the "fountain of hope." He is the source of true hope. If we remain surrendered to his ways, the leading of the Spirit will grow us up in the ways of God. We know how the Spirit works through the evidence of his fruit in our lives. Following him affects everything we do, including how we think about the future. If we are aligned in his hope, we walk with courage and confidence in his love, knowing he will lead us into the life of his eternal kingdom.

We can follow the impulses of the Holy Spirit in our lives, even today. The Spirit moves in loving-awareness. Compassion compels us and joy lifts our spirits. The Spirit does not motivate us in fear, but in mercy-kindness. Remember this, and you will be able to test what is good, pure, and true.

Yield yourself to the love of God and ask the Spirit to lead you in big and small ways today. Be intentional about leaning in to hear his voice.

Good Works

He has told you, O man, what is good;
and what does the LORD require of you but to do justice,
and to love kindness, and to walk humbly with your God?

MICAH 6:8 ESV

The requirements of God throughout the ages have not changed. When we love the Lord with our hearts, minds, souls, and strength, and we love our neighbor as ourselves, the end result becomes doing justice, loving kindness, and walking humbly with our God. Love covers a multitude of wrongs. When we humble ourselves before God, we cannot ignore that to be like him means choosing kindness, treating others with respect, and standing on the side of justice.

Our lives reveal where our hope lies. If we prioritize status over loving action, we show that our hope is in what we can gain on this earth. We cannot control how others may choose to live, but we can direct our own lives with the placement of our hope and the follow through of our actions. Let's do good works in love, as God requires of us, not because we must, but because there is so much reward in it.

What does your life and choices reveal about where your hope lies? Determine if you need to adjust your priorities or approach to others to be more in line with what you want to be true.

Clothed in Kindness

As God's chosen ones, holy and dearly loved, put on compassion, kindness, humility, gentleness, and patience.

COLOSSIANS 3:12 CSB

Compassion may not come naturally to us, but that does not mean that we can't clothe ourselves in it. We don't have to be born with humility to grow in it. We can struggle with patience and still choose it! There are stages in our lives (even developmentally) where it is harder to initially choose these things. In these times we learn how to fail and to choose differently. The same is true for our spirituality.

When we choose to clothe ourselves in compassion, kindness, humility, gentleness, and patience, we put on the nature of God. We aim to be like him. Beloved, it does take choice. He's not looking for perfection, but a willingness to learn and grow in character. What hope there is as we put our effort and faith together!

In every interaction, choose to put on compassion, kindness, humility, gentleness, and patience. And when you don't, be quick to adjust and do better.

Ready for Challenges

"When you go through deep waters,
I will be with you.
When you go through rivers of difficulty,
you will not drown.
When you walk through the fire of oppression,
you will not be burned up;
the flames will not consume you."

ISAIAH 43:2 NLT

The promise of God's presence with us can be enough to turn our anxiety into hope. The Lord told his people not to be afraid. Why should we not give into fear even when faced with fierce storms? Because we belong to the Lord, he has called us by name, and he goes with us into every fire.

If we do not expect to come up against challenges in this life, we will be sorely disillusioned when they do come our way. We can't avoid them! But in every one, the Lord promises us his presence. He sees us, knows us, and goes with us in mercy. His love never lets up, and his grace never leaves. With God as our source and strength, we can be ready to face whatever comes!

When you put your hope in the Lord, it won't disappoint. Align your expectations with the power of God's grace and remember that he called you before you even knew his name!

Momentary Troubles

Our momentary, light affliction is producing for us an eternal weight of glory far beyond all comparison.

2 Corinthians 4:17 nasb

Every trial is temporary. Even our greatest afflictions will come to an end. As we keep this in mind, that hope can help us in resilience and perseverance through hard times. Hope has been found to be an effective intervention, especially in youth, for mental health struggles. Each of us will go through trying times, but when we do, hope can keep us from despair. Hope reminds us that the hard is not all that exists; there is goodness and possibility, too.

When heartbreak or grief comes crashing into our lives, the ease of happier days can feel like a distant memory. Hope doesn't rely on happiness, though, and it doesn't depend on ease. Hope is most powerful in our greatest challenges. Though it may seem simple, a perspective shift can be enough to move us from darkness to light, and from despair to hope.

You have survived every single hard thing that has come your way this far, and you will continue to get through today. Remember that troubles are temporary, but the mercy of God is eternal.

Good of Others

Each of us should please our neighbors for their good,
to build them up.

ROMANS 15:2 NIV

If we are not careful, we may become overly self-focused. It is okay to have our preferences and priorities, but if we don't also serve others in love, we may find ourselves apathetic to the lives of those around us. We should encourage our neighbors and build them up, taking their perspectives and needs into account.

We cannot escape the importance of relationships in our lives, and not only those of our family members and friends. We need interaction with casual acquaintances, too. As we show kindness and honor through seeking to build them up in love, we get outside of our own heads for a while. This helps to broaden our perspectives and can make us more empathetic and understanding of those who are different than us. What does this have to do with hope? These connections can give us inspiration, make us think in new ways, and deepen our sense of belonging in the world, which all lends to optimistic possibilities.

Consider how you can be of help to the people around you today. When you see an opportunity, fill it.

Process of Transformation

We all, with unveiled face, beholding as in a mirror the glory of the Lord, are being transformed into the same image from glory to glory, just as by the Spirit of the Lord.

2 CORINTHIANS 3:18 NKJV

Over time, we become like what we focus on. Our attention is powerful, so it is in our best interest to be intentional about where we direct it. If we want to be more like Christ, we cannot ignore the importance of spending time with him. Reading through the gospels are a practical way to get to know what Jesus is like. Spending time in prayer, deepening our friendship with the Holy Spirit is also important.

The more we direct our attention to the Lord, the greater our chance of becoming like him. But this doesn't happen by accident. We must be purposeful. Transformation takes time, but it also takes effort. Consistency is key. But even in all of this, the grace of God is ours. We have the help of the Holy Spirit to do far more than we could on our own. Let's lean into that grace and invite the Spirit to move our hearts, even as we fix our thoughts on him.

What kind of transformation do you want to see happen in your life? What can you do to move in that direction today?

Beautiful Thoughts

Think about the things that are good and worthy of praise.
Think about the things that are true and honorable and
right and pure and beautiful and respected.

PHILIPPIANS 4:8 NCV

We can transform the terrain of our minds by choosing what
kinds of things we will dwell on. Though we cannot control
every thought that enters our mind, we certainly can decide
which ones we entertain. Instead of judging our thoughts as
reflections of our worth, when we learn to approach them with
curiosity, shame cannot keep us from the liberty of God's love
and the ability that is ours to take our thoughts captive.

We don't have to hate our thoughts to redirect them. We
don't have to demean ourselves when we are caught thinking
something that is not how we want to think. As we submit
our hearts and minds to Christ, he renews us. We can partner
with his mercy and choose a better way; we can choose better
thoughts. As we do, we may find that hope comes more easily.

*Take stock of your thoughts and consider the fruit of them.
Are they producing the kind of person that you want to be?
Use today's verse to choose how you direct your thoughts
today.*

Hopeful Fixation

Set your gaze on the path before you.
With fixed purpose, looking straight ahead,
ignore life's distractions.

PROVERBS 4:25 TPT

To achieve our goals and move toward hope, we must know what they are. When we have nothing to work toward, we may feel aimless and devoid of purpose in life.

We can have many hopes, but they must be something that we can make steps toward. Even if they seem impossible and far off now, there are steps we can take today to get closer to them. Then, as we continue to implement consistency, we gain momentum. It all begins with a vision. As we set our gaze on the path before us, we fixate on the purpose and can ignore life's distractions, as we do!

Do you know what you're working toward in your life at the moment? It doesn't have to feel earth shattering. It can be simple. If you find that your goals are too small, consider dreaming bigger. Be sure you know what you are working toward so that you don't become distracted by everything along the way.

An Open Table

Live in harmony with one another.
Do not be haughty, but associate with the lowly.
Never be wise in your own sight.

ROMANS 12:16 ESV

The kingdom of Christ is not a club. It is a family. We don't get to choose our brothers and sisters, but we are called to love them. Cultivating a humble heart can help us in resisting divisions, including those that fall on class distinctions, ethnic differences, and simply our personal preferences. Although it's not our responsibility to be close to everyone in our lives, it certainly is to be kind.

If we are going to err one way or the other, it would serve us well to choose to associate with the lowly. When we spend our time and energy on trying to impress powerful people, we don't have the freedom to love and serve those who need it most. Choosing kindness promotes a hopeful attitude in those who receive it, and in those who extend it.

Be a promoter of peace in your neighborhood by showing kindness to those who others ignore.

A Different Way

Since the weapons of our warfare are not of the flesh, but are powerful through God for the demolition of strongholds. We demolish arguments and every proud thing that is raised up against the knowledge of God, and we take every thought captive to obey Christ.

2 CORINTHIANS 10:4-5 CSB

There is so much fighting in this world. We are not to war against each other with weapons, or even with threats. God calls us to a different way. We demolish arguments by refusing to argue. We humble ourselves in love and let that be our covering. We don't simply let ourselves get carried away by fear, anger, or retribution. As we follow the Lord in his love, we lay down our need to prove ourselves right and instead do what is before us to do.

If our hope is that we will never be wrong, or even that all people will like us, we cannot live with integrity. We will avoid our own faults or hide parts of ourselves from others. We have been called to the liberty of God's love. Our hope, firmly anchored in him, allows us to live truly, with one focus—on his ways. When we mess up, we can start again.

Instead of engaging with arguments that lead nowhere, let them go. Focus on what is yours to do, living with kindness and love.

Helpful Thoughts

Those who are dominated by the sinful nature think about sinful things, but those who are controlled by the Holy Spirit think about things that please the Spirit.

ROMANS 8:5 NLT

Hope lives in the realm of our thoughts. It keeps us moving in action toward it. Our thoughts are important to not only monitor, but to take action in our own hearts, minds, and lives. If we want to do better, we must not neglect the power of thinking better.

Friendship with the Holy Spirit helps us to see things in a different way. Just like our friends can influence our attitudes and tendencies, so does the powerful perspective of the Spirit. If we want to grow in heavenly hope, deepening our relationship with God is an incredibly important way to do this. The more we know him, the more confidence we gain in his faithfulness. His wisdom affects our expectation and understanding. We can't ignore this impact.

Meditate on the Holy Spirit and the fruit of his presence (found in Galatians 5). Ask for his perspective. The more you do, the more your thoughts will transform in the wisdom of God.

July

God wanted to make known among
the Gentiles the glorious wealth
of this mystery, which is Christ in you,
the hope of glory.

COLOSSIANS 1:27 CSB

Daring to Be Different

Not all people have this knowledge;
but some, being accustomed to the idol until now,
eat food as if it were sacrificed to an idol;
and their conscience, being weak, is defiled.

1 CORINTHIANS 8:7 NASB

Being able to think differently is an incredible advantage in life, and that is also true for our hope. The ability to see from different perspectives, seeing different options where others are entrenched in sameness and wanting to fit in, is a strength.

Questioning the way things are, the status quo, can lead us to eventual breakthrough. This is not without challenge. We should not prioritize sameness over authenticity. If we do, not only do systems suffer, but we, as individuals, do, too. Just because we've adopted traditions, even within our religious systems, does not mean that those traditions reflect the heart of God. It doesn't mean that it is what God wants for us. Knowing God—his character, his ways, and his heart—is more important than knowing the particulars of rites and rituals. They have their place, but they shouldn't be considered more important than God, himself, or who he says that we are.

If you have questions about why things are done the way they are; don't shrink back. God welcomes your questions, and he has given you freedom!

It's Not Insignificant

"Truly I tell you, whatever you did for one of the least of these brothers and sisters of mine, you did for me."

MATTHEW 25:40 NIV

Everyone is welcome in the kingdom of the Lord. Jesus said to let the children come freely to him. He spent time with tax collectors (who were hated in their day), and he healed those who were sick, tormented, and outcasts of society. No one was beneath him. We should take the same attitude, recognizing that when we serve the least of these, we serve Christ himself.

Every movement made in mercy and compassion is a movement made toward the Lord. He honors our service and sacrifice, no matter how little it may seem to us. No small act of kindness goes unnoticed! Let's fill our days, then, with openhearted generosity to all people, but especially to those who need it the most.

Your actions can inspire hope in others. Be generous with your time, attention, and resources today. Be intentional in kindness, even if the act seems small to you.

Shift Your Attention

I will lift up my eyes to the hills—
From whence comes my help?
My help comes from the Lord,
Who made heaven and earth.

PSALM 121:1-2 NKJV

When we lift our eyes to the landscape around us and see nothing, it as an opportunity to shift our gaze toward hope. Sometimes we need the reminder that our help doesn't begin and end with those around us; it is ultimately in the Lord! His ways are higher and his faithfulness more reliable than any other. Even if no one else comes to our aid, God most certainly will.

We can rest assured that the one who never slumbers will not overlook us in our need. He is the one who keeps us. He really is faithful, and we can trust him. Let's shift our attention from our circumstances, then, and onto the one who is loyal and powerful to save!

When you can't tell how you're going to get through something, turn your attention to the Lord and ask for the reassurance of his presence and help.

A New Path

"Look at the new thing I am going to do.
It is already happening. Don't you see it?
I will make a road in the desert and rivers in the dry land."

ISAIAH 43:19 NCV

God is never stagnant or at a loss for what to do. He is always up to something new. Every sunrise is a fresh start and a unique expression of God's faithfulness. Though the Lord never changes, he also never stops moving in mercy and innovation. If we resist the transformation that comes with new discoveries, we resist the very essence of who God created us to be. We are to be continuously learning and growing in understanding. No two days are the same, and that is as true for our lives as it is for the world.

We shouldn't be surprised when we find a new thing unfolding before us. Hope is to be ever before us. Small changes over time add up to big transformations. We should take a proactive approach, then, in where we set our hope, what we do with it, and how we walk it out. Don't worry; this isn't a call for perfection. It's a call to inspiration and a commitment to following the Lord through it all.

If you are feeling stuck in any area of your life, ask the Lord to show you where he is calling you into in a new way. He makes roads through deserts, so no challenge is too great for him!

Good Shepherd

Yahweh is my best friend and my shepherd.
I always have more than enough.

PSALM 23:1 TPT

In the presence of God, we find rest for our souls. This isn't
something we have to wait for, either; it is something we can
experience here and now as the Spirit of God washes over us.
Our worth isn't found in what we do for God, it's found in who
he says we are, who he always created us to be.

Deepening our relationship with our God is an active
commitment to being the best people we can be. We find
ourselves loved to life in his presence, time and again. Being
our best doesn't mean never experiencing weakness or failure.
It means that we turn to God through it all. We allow his love
to challenge and change us, to motivate us and be our source.
In him, we always have more than enough, for his resources
are endless!

*Keep an open connection with the Lord in your heart today
and ask him to lead you, to refresh you, and to speak to you
throughout your day.*

Redirected Energy

Let not your heart envy sinners,
but continue in the fear of the Lord all the day.

PROVERBS 23:17 ESV

When we direct our passion toward the Lord, we can focus the strength of our emotions on him. Instead of becoming overcome by envy or anger toward others, we can redirect that emotional energy toward the Lord. As we do, we are more able to let go and trust him with the things that aren't in our power to change.

Consider the last time you were frustrated by a situation completely out of your control. How much energy did you expend on it? It's not that we aren't meant to feel things strongly; there is wisdom in knowing when we can do something about it and when we can't, to take it to the Lord and surrender it. As we do, our hearts and minds are freed up to focus on what we can do to make a difference.

How often do you find yourself preoccupied with things completely out of your control? When you feel yourself reacting to somebody or something, direct that energy in prayer, and ask for the Lord to give you wisdom in letting go of what is not yours to carry.

Invaluable

The LORD values those who fear him,
those who put their hope in his faithful love.

PSALM 147:11 CSB

The Lord values those who submit their lives to him. This value is not transactional, either. God *delights*, or takes pleasure in, those who fear him. We are invaluable to the Lord. If we question this truth, all we must do is look at Christ and his sacrifice. God has always cherished relationship with us. Love was his motivation at the beginning, and it remains his motivation today.

Research shows that those who have secure attachments within their relationships have higher levels of hope and happiness. Though we cannot control the families that we are born into, we can know the love and delight of God as it transforms our hearts, our thoughts, and our expectations. God's love is more secure than any other, for he never withholds it or manipulates us. We are invaluable to God simply because we are his children.

Ask the Lord to show you his delight over you. As he reveals his incredible kindness, pour out your own delight back unto him. This is the beauty of worship. We receive freely, and from that, we offer it back to the Lord.

Incredible Peace

Since we have been made right in God's sight by faith, we have peace with God because of what Jesus Christ our Lord has done for us.

ROMANS 5:1 NLT

Ongoing stress has effects, not only on our emotional and mental wellbeing, but on our physical bodies, too. Research shows that toxic (ongoing) stress affects development in children. This is serious business! This ongoing stress is usually in response to a heightened nervous system as a result of trauma. But even those who have experienced great distress have hope. There are tools, such as intergenerational approaches, that offer support and help to relieve the stress. Those with strong levels of support can weather these circumstances knowing that they are not alone in them.

Sometimes, simply the acknowledgment and naming of our trauma can bring relief. Being seen in our struggles can be enough to not make us feel alone anymore. Often, as we share these things, we find that we are not the only ones who experience these things. Graciously, there is peace for each of us, not only in the solace and support of others, but in Christ and what he has done.

If you are struggling, reach out to someone you trust and share it. Also, pray for peace. God's Spirit is ever so near, and he won't fail to connect you with the right people.

Great Confidence

Having such a hope, we use great boldness in our speech, and we are not like Moses, who used to put a veil over his face so that the sons of Israel would not stare at the end of what was fading away.

2 CORINTHIANS 3:12-13 NASB

When we are sure of our hope, our confidence grows. If we don't believe that our hopes can become reality, however, then we may find ourselves shrinking in conviction. It is as important that we believe what we are working toward is possible as it is to have the hope itself.

Hope gives us something to work toward, believing that it's worth it. Confidence is what makes us put in the work. Without confidence, we will never take the action necessary to push beyond our own limitations. Our hopes may seem far off, but confidence helps us to break it down into manageable steps without getting bogged down by the distance between our hope and our current reality.

Is there a gap between your hope and confidence to put it into action? Consider what has been holding you back. Perhaps you need a shift in mindset, the self-discipline to do something, however small, about it today, or a different hope, altogether. Do what aligns for you today.

As for Me

As for me, I watch in hope for the LORD,
I wait for God my Savior; my God will hear me.

MICAH 7:7 NIV

Choosing to engage in hope is up to us. It is a choice that we each must make for ourselves. Although we can grow in hope through the encouragement of others, we must opt to *watch in hope* in our own hearts, minds, and lives.

According to Hope Theory, as coined by C. R. Snyder, hope has three elements: goals, willpower, and pathways. Goals are the cornerstones of hope. Willpower is the ability to keep moving toward goals in motivation, believing the end will be worth it. Pathways are the routes we take to meet our goals. They often are not straight paths; people with high levels of hope tend to recognize that roadblocks are unavoidable, and it may take different approaches to achieve goals. Knowing willpower is a key component of hope, we must take an active role in making them a reality!

Active waiting is an important concept. Waiting does not mean you have no work to do or steps you can take toward goals. Be sure to approach the in-between times with knowledge that you (and you alone) can choose how you wait.

Secure in Hope

You would be secure, because there is hope;
Yes, you would dig around you,
and take your rest in safety.

JOB 11:18 NKJV

If we direct our hearts to God and surrender to him, we allow his love to pierce our hearts. As he reveals what in our lives contradicts his merciful ways, we can redirect our thoughts and actions to align with him. We can remove the things that stand against God's ways. He offers us liberty in his lavish love; there is nothing that we can't overcome with his help!

In all things, especially in areas where we see the need for change, hope is paramount. If we believe that transformation is possible, we have hope. If we feel as if there are no options for us, then we need a fresh encounter with the presence of God that reveals the paths of righteousness, which is reason to hope, indeed. God offers redemption, renewal, and rest for all who depend on him.

If there is something in your life that feels doomed, ask the Lord for his hopeful insight. In him, there is always an alternative that leads to peace.

Man of His Word

God is not a human being, and he will not lie. He is not a human, and he does not change his mind. What he says he will do, he does. What he promises, he makes come true.

NUMBERS 23:19 NCV

God does not lie. Though we cannot know if others are always telling us the truth, we can rest assured that God never deceives us. He doesn't twist the truth or try to manipulate a situation by omitting important facts. He is always true, always righteous, and forever faithful. He cannot be caught in a lie because he simply does not tell them. Though we may struggle to believe those who have broken our trust, may we only grow stronger and more confident in Christ as he follows faithfully through on all he has said.

Knowing that God does not lie (nor does he have the need to), we can also rest assured that we don't have to read his mind. We can take him at his word. What confident hope we have when we know that we can rely on him!

Do your best to be honest and true. Don't say what you don't mean, and when you do, admit to it and right the wrong. Integrity is a high value of the kingdom. Ask God for his help to follow through and be reliable to your own word.

Power of Encouragement

I am convinced that my God will fully satisfy every need
you have, for I have seen the abundant riches of glory
revealed to me through Jesus Christ!

PHILIPPIANS 4:19 TPT

The encouragement of others can be just the motivation we
need to keep going in hope. Though we are the only ones
who can truly choose hope, a timely encouragement can
make all the difference in a hard time. The apostle Paul often
encouraged the readers in his letters. Let's not neglect the
power of an uplifting word in our own relationships.

When we are specific and intentional with others about what
we appreciate about them, it can be like a balm of peace
and an infusion of confidence to them. Sometimes when we
are in the midst of a significant challenge, it can be hard to
remember the good things. Hardship can feel all consuming.
We were created for relationship and for the support it brings.
Encouragement through an intentional comment, an act of
service, or a hug, can offer strength.

*Reach out to someone with the intention of encouraging
them. Don't make it up or be generic; be specific, and most of
all let them know that they are loved.*

Hope for Justice

O Lord, you hear the desire of the afflicted;
you will strengthen their heart;
you will incline your ear to do justice
to the fatherless and the oppressed,
so that man who is of the earth
may strike terror no more.

PSALM 10:17–18 ESV

One of the most disheartening experiences in this world is to watch injustice occur without recourse. It can feel utterly exhausting to realize that there doesn't seem to be true accountability for some who commit wrongdoings. If our only hope for justice is in this world and its systems, we will be sorely disappointed.

God hears the vulnerable and their cries. He does not favor the powerful or protect their egos. If we want to be found on the side of the Lord and his ways, we should do as he said in Micah 6:8: "to do justice, and to love kindness, and to walk humbly with your God." This is the good way. Justice is judging people fairly, without partiality. Even if we do our best and fail, God will never fail from being the perfect judge.

Hope removes the feeling of helplessness because it sees a path forward. Set your hope on Christ and follow his lead in justice, even while you wait on his.

Endurance through Hope

Blessed is the one who endures trials, because when he has stood the test he will receive the crown of life that God has promised to those who love him.

JAMES 1:12 CSB

Endurance is directly linked to our hope. Though trials come, when we know the hope we have –the promise and possibility of what we are working toward; we can hold on and stay the course. Patience is required of all of us. Though we live in a world where we can find instant answers and services at our fingertips, the challenges of life do not work this way. We cannot wish away our grief or skip a recovery process. We need to learn the gift of endurance, for it will teach and refine us if we let it.

When we have hope, we can self-regulate and make sacrifices in the present for the benefit of our goals. Endurance works in a similar way. When trials test our resolve, we can find courage and resilience in the hope we hold onto. Perseverance is a strength in life, and we can all grow in it. Finding encouragement from Scriptures, from community support, and from God himself, we can keep pressing on while not losing hope.

Set a goal for the day and keep bringing it to mind when you feel tempted to give up.

Light in the Darkness

The light shines in the darkness,
and the darkness can never extinguish it.

JOHN 1:5 NLT

Hope is like a light in a dark room. It illuminates the shadows and gives us the ability to see what is around us, even if the room itself remains dim. Even a small flicker of light makes darkness flee and brings peace and confidence in the ability to make out what was once a mystery.

The unknown is a lot like a dark void: the mystery of it can feel overwhelming. However, when a light reveals what was hidden, the fear of the unknown often dissipates. When we can see the ground beneath our feet, the steps we take are more confident. Jesus is the light that brightens our darkest days. Nothing is a mystery to him, so let's trust him to guide us in his goodness through every hill and valley of this life.

Even a small flicker of light can bring understanding. Ask the Spirit to reveal a step that you can take toward your hope today.

Lacking Nothing

The young lions do without and suffer hunger;
But they who seek the LORD will not lack any good thing.

PSALM 34:10 NASB

The promises of God are yes and amen. He vows to provide for his children. When we are in need, it is an opportunity to lean into the nearness of God and trust him to provide. There will also be opportunities we have to partner with him and his ways in active faith. This reflects our hope. He is a good God who cares for his children, and he is also a wonderful source that offers us the satisfaction of reaping the fruit of our labor.

There are some needs that can be easily met by sharing them with others. There are others that are met by us doing the work that is in front of us to do. Still, there are other needs that lay completely outside of our control. No matter the case, our trust and hope can remain in God, our good Father. As we seek the Lord, we will not lack any good thing!

Take time throughout your day to seek the Lord, whether through prayer, Scripture, or fellowship. Every time you are inspired in hope, thank him!

Resisting Discouragement

"The LORD himself goes before you and will be with you;
he will never leave you nor forsake you.
Do not be afraid; do not be discouraged."

DEUTERONOMY 31:8 NIV

How is it that we resist perpetual discouragement in our lives? If we remember the powerful presence of God and the promises of God to his people, we can draw on the hope that they bring, rather than spending all our efforts focusing on the problems we face. When we feel discouraged, we should not heap shame upon ourselves; this is a part of life. It is staying in discouragement that will make us stuck.

God reminds us (as many times as it takes) that his love is present with us. His mercy is inescapable. Though we must face the problems in our lives, he promises to go before us and to be with us in them. This is where hope helps us take courage! With God's help, we have all that we need for whatever comes our way. He will never leave or forsake us, so we don't have to give in to fear!

When you begin to feel overwhelmed by what lies ahead, remind yourself of the promise that the Lord himself goes before you. What remains a mystery to you is clear to him! Let your hope rest in the nearness of his presence in every moment.

Consider It

What then shall we say to these things?
If God is for us, who can be against us?

ROMANS 8:31 NKJV

God's love triumphs over all. No matter where we go, God is with us. Even when we are in uncharted territory, the Lord knows it like the back of his hand. God has chosen us as his children before we were even formed in the womb. In love, he created us. In goodness, he knit us together. He himself has justified us through Christ. As we yield our lives to him, we are covered by his mercy. We are renewed, redeemed, and filled with the gracious generosity of his love all the days of our lives.

Considering this, why we would we fear anyone in this world? We are as able to walk in the confident love of Christ as anyone else. No one is excluded or invalidated. All are welcome in the kingdom of Christ. Let's not forget that choosing the path of love is a privilege, and not a burden. There are treasures beyond what we could imagine lining the path, and so much more in the fullness of God's kingdom that awaits us.

Spend time remembering who God says you are and who he has called you to be. Don't overlook the power of God's work in you. In an act of faith, reach out to help someone who needs it, remembering that God does that for you.

Importance of Fellowship

Every time I pray. I pray that I will be allowed to come to you, and this will happen if God wants it. I want very much to see you, to give you some spiritual gift to make you strong.

ROMANS 1:10-11 NCV

The power of community cannot be overstated in our levels of hope. Those with support systems in place can build resilience and grow their hope. If it is difficult to get through a single day, however, it can be impossible to plan. We need the exchange of support that happens in meaningful relationships.

In community, we may find tools that we didn't even know were available when we were simply trying to get by on our own. We grow in hope when we know that we have a safety net. For some, this may be their family. For others, it may be community programs. Still, for others, the safety network of connections they find to strengthen their resolve is in spiritual fellowship and belonging at a church. Wherever we find it, we must remember that we don't thrive in isolation, but in secure relationships.

Make it a priority to spend time in meaningful connection with others throughout your week. They don't all have to be deep either.

Now to Him

To the one with enough power to prevent you from stumbling into sin and bring you faultless before his glorious presence to stand before him with ecstatic delight, to the only God our Savior, through our Lord Jesus Christ, be endless glory and majesty, great power and authority—from before he created time, now, and throughout all the ages of eternity.

JUDE 1:24-25 TPT

Just because we feel hope for something does not mean that it is always easy to choose. On the contrary, there will be times when hope feels hard. God is with us in the struggle, but that doesn't mean that we lose our ability to choose. Who of us cannot relate to struggling to choose positivity when we are tired, hungry, or simply frustrated? Hope will not always feel be easy to choose, but that doesn't mean it's not worth it.

The Lord's power is greater than we know. He can prevent us from stumbling into sin by covering us in the all-sufficient mercy of his own heart. Christ's sacrifice was all that was necessary to purify us before the Father. We can come boldly before the throne of grace and ask the Lord to renew and refresh our hearts whenever we need it.

Your negative feelings don't have to define you. Choose to lean on the Lord and his grace today, whether or not you are in the mood to.

Delicious Delight

Rejoice in the Lord always;
again I will say, rejoice.

PHILIPPIANS 4:4 ESV

In every season, we can choose to rejoice in the Lord. Joy is not predicated on our circumstances. We don't have to be happy, even, to choose joy. While happiness is often an emotional response to something, joy is an internal contentment found in the satisfaction of the present moment. It is consistent and eternal, rather than being a temporary feeling. We can tune into this joy through purposeful connection to the Lord and his presence with us.

As we delight ourselves in the Lord, we choose to rejoice in who he is at all times. His nature never shifts or wavers. He is always faithful, always good, and always true. He won't leave us, and he won't give us stones when we ask for bread. He is always better than we expect, and he won't ever let us down. What delicious delight we find in the abundant peace, hope, love, and joy of his presence!

Write down five to ten reasons you can think of to rejoice in the Lord today. Get as granular as you like; the little things count as much as the big!

Choose It

Though you have not seen him, you love him;
though not seeing him now, you believe in him,
and you rejoice with inexpressible and glorious joy.

1 PETER 1:8 CSB

Hope is distinct from wishing and optimism. It is not a singular concept that can be wrapped up and packaged for wholesale. It is a tool that all people can use, and there are different types of hope that we can harness. In every season and situation that comes, hope remains a choice.

Hope is a resource that helps us find solutions to problems, manage our own personal struggles, and helps us to reach toward the future with purpose. Research reveals that those with high hope levels can weather the storms of life with more resilience. No matter our level of hope at any moment, we can grow in our capacity to hope by choosing it and by remaining connected to others. Though our hopes may take on different shapes throughout our lives, the power of hope's perspective helps us to move through difficulties.

Hope is greater than optimism because it doesn't require positive thinking all the time. Be honest with your feelings today and see how hope can help you manage them.

Nourishing Words

When I discovered your words, I devoured them. They are
my joy and my heart's delight, for I bear your name, O LORD
God of Heaven's Armies.

JEREMIAH 15:16 NLT

Encouragement is vital to our resolve. We will not always wake
up to a new day feeling ready for whatever it throws at us. Some
mornings may bring a struggle to even get out of bed. Our
souls need nourishment as much as our bodies do. We must not
neglect the nutrition our hearts, minds, and spirits need.

Hope makes a difference. If we need more hope, we can find
encouragement in the testimonies of others that persevered
through hard times. These can be found in Scripture, but also,
they can be found all around us. There are heroes of hope
within recent history, but we may have someone close to us
that we look up to in this regard, as well. Let's not neglect the
power of encouragement we can find in the lived experiences
of others.

*Read or listen to a personal story of hope through hard times. If
you know someone who you want to know more of their story,
have a conversation about it. Whatever brings encouragement,
hope, or peace to your soul is a nourishing word.*

Dwell in Love

"If you keep My commandments, you will remain in My love; just as I have kept My Father's commandments and remain in His love."

JOHN 15:10 NASB

Love is found in connection to others. When we choose to dwell in the love of God, we intentionally clothe ourselves in his ways. We don't prefer our opinions over others' wellbeing. Love motivates us to walk alongside others and offer them the support that we also need in our own lives.

If we have hope, we should be intentional about offering our own strategies and skills to those without it. If we have any success in our lives, we should be willing to share how we got there with others. This is a part of love—to be generous. We love because God first loved us. He offers us all the wisdom we need, and he never withholds goodness from those who ask for it. Let's be as gracious with our resources as God is with us!

Offer to help someone who needs it today. Whether with tools, a reference, or a few bucks, be generous in love, knowing that it reflects God's graciousness toward you!

A Spacious Place

When hard pressed, I cried to the LORD;
he brought me into a spacious place.

PSALM 118:5 NIV

When we are hard pressed in life, we need the relief that space brings. Tidal waves of grief can crash into our lives and leave us gasping for air. Unforeseen challenges can turn a beloved space into what feels like a prison cell. What once seemed a promising future can become a dead end. The gracious thing about God is that he doesn't leave us to be crushed in or by our circumstances. No ending is final; there is always an opportunity for a fresh start and an expansion of understanding.

We need not be afraid to call on the Lord for help. He is ready and willing to help us whenever we cry out to him! We can take refuge in him whenever the storms of life threaten us. He is ever so good to us, and he won't leave us out in the cold. He brings us from the confined places of our trouble into the spaciousness of his presence where we can find our rest. He renews and refreshes us, and he offers us perspective that we couldn't see on our own.

When you feel closed in by the troubles of life, call on the Lord. His peace brings space, light, and expansion to your heart and soul. There is a spacious place in his presence, no matter where you are!

Unifying Hope

If there is any consolation in Christ, if any comfort of love, if any fellowship of the Spirit, if any affection and mercy, fulfill my joy by being like-minded, having the same love, being of one accord, of one mind.

PHILIPPIANS 2:1-2 NKJV

Hope can unify us in purpose and determination. A shared hope is a shared motivation to a specific end. Each of us can take part in seeing change because we believe that change is possible. This is why hope is such a powerful force in our lives, as well as in many programs. Without hope for recovery, for instance, there would be little to motivate those in programs to help overcome addictions.

Though many of our hopes may remain personal, it is good to engage with greater hope that unifies us as people. With one overarching goal, we can see meaningful change take place through our efforts. Hope is powerful in one life, but it is exponential in a movement!

Volunteer for an organization that promotes a cause that you believe in. Where there is hope for goodness in this world, there is opportunity to sow into it!

Wrapped in Goodness

The LORD makes me very happy; all that I am rejoices in my God. He has covered me with clothes of salvation and wrapped me with a coat of goodness, like a bridegroom dressed for his wedding, like a bride dressed in jewels.

ISAIAH 61:10 NCV

We cannot live in the past, but we can draw encouragement, hope, and strength from it. As we recall how goodness and mercy have met us in our lives, we ground ourselves in the reality of their impact. If all we ever do is remember the hard and painful times, we rob ourselves of the beauty of the glimmers of goodness as it met us. If, on the other hand, we only remember the light and fluffy things, we may miss out on the lessons of resilience within the hard times. There is beauty and nourishment in it all.

Perhaps where these two overlap is where the most joy is found. Every difficulty is an opportunity to expand in understanding and grow in grace. Where did God meet us through the hills and valleys we have already traveled? As we see the glimpses of his mercy, let's give him our heartfelt thanks for all he has done, and look with hope to all that he will continue to do.

Use your own history as a place to explore where God's goodness has met you. Ask the Spirit to give you eyes to see where God's love was all along.

Expansive Expectations

If the only benefit of our hope in Christ is limited to this life on earth, we deserve to be pitied more than all others!

1 CORINTHIANS 15:19 TPT

If we limit the scope of our hope to our own lives, we remain too small-minded! Our lives and choices ripple. Our foresight can be a blessing to others. We must consider how our choices affect the generations that follow. This world is our home for a time, but it is also home to millions more. If we remain disconnected from the importance our choices have on others, we remain self-focused and ignorant to the ways we could choose to breathe hope into others through our honorable efforts.

If our expectations and hopes remain about us and our benefit alone, we are missing the power of God's kingdom and the promise of his redemption to all who call on him. Let's dare to expand our expectations to what good we could do in the world, and to the glory that awaits us beyond it.

Consider a hope that extends beyond your own life. How can you meaningfully grow in sowing into it?

Joyful Hope

The hope of the righteous brings joy,
but the expectation of the wicked will perish.

PROVERBS 10:28 ESV

Hope is purposeful; it gives us awareness of what we are working toward. It breathes possibility into our dreams and awakens our hearts to what we have yet to experience. If we don't have vision for something, we won't know to move toward it with our actions. Before we have hope, we also need to feel the need for it. If there isn't a challenge or lack in our lives, hope isn't necessary.

Once we are aware of something, we can do something about it. Without awareness, we don't realize the opportunity we have to act. God's promises give us hope, but they also clarify our needs in a way that causes us to take God at his word. There is joy in putting our hope in God and in aligning our lifestyles with his love.

Pray and ask the Lord to show you a hope that you can move toward with your choices today. If you struggle to hear from him, look at the areas where you feel a lack of motivation, and find where the promises of God can meet you in it.

Success with the Lord

Unless the LORD builds a house,
its builders labor over it in vain;
unless the LORD watches over a city,
the watchman stays alert in vain.

PSALM 127:1 CSB

The grace of God empowers us to build things that last. God is a gracious provider, and he can do far more than we can imagine. It does us no use to overwork ourselves for fear of not having enough. Never giving ourselves margin for rest and play does nothing but burn us out. God did not create us to work from sunup until sundown. There are rhythms to life, and this includes rest and renewal.

When we yield our hearts to the Lord, he blesses the work of our hands. As we partner with his purposes, he uses our offerings and increases their influence. He can do this and so much more. Let's be sure to build balance within our lives, leaving time for the people and things that bring us joy and peace. We can trust that the Lord blesses our work, but we certainly don't have to become workaholics to please him; remember it is by grace we have been saved through faith. We don't earn our place in his kingdom through striving.

Commit your work to the Lord and give yourself the freedom and permission to take your rest and play just as seriously!

August

I pray that your hearts will be flooded with light so that you can understand the confident hope he has given to those he called— his holy people who are his rich and glorious inheritance.

EPHESIANS 1:18 NLT

Secure Wisdom

Those who trust their own insight are foolish,
but anyone who walks in wisdom is safe.

PROVERBS 28:26 NLT

If the extent of our confidence lies within our own means and knowledge, then at some point, we will be disappointed. Wisdom recognizes that we are limited in our scope, but it also acknowledges that we can learn and grow from every opportunity, both in triumph and in failure.

Those who are wise in their own eyes may seem competent and secure, but true wisdom is found in humility and the willingness to admit when we get it wrong. A façade of strength is different than a house built upon a firm foundation. Let's be sure that we focus more on the wisdom of God, allowing ourselves to expand in our understanding as we learn from our mistakes and listen to the input of wise ones around us. There is security in wisdom, but those who claim to know it all are on shaky ground.

Be willing to admit when you don't know something and be intentional in being open to the wisdom and discernment of others, especially those who have been in your position.

Rich Hope

Know that wisdom is the same for your soul;
If you find it, then there will be a future,
And your hope will not be cut off.

PROVERBS 24:14 NASB

Hope is found in wisdom because wisdom meets us in the practicalities of life. Hope is not simply a far-off ideal. It is a goal, and every goal has a path to get there. Wisdom gives us eyes to see the steps in that direction.

Hope fuels our souls with rich nourishment. It keeps us moving toward wisdom with belief and desire. The more we taste and see the goodness of God in the wisdom of his Word playing out in our lives, the more our hope grows. The more our hope grows, the more we are motivated to walk in wisdom's ways. It is a cyclical path that builds momentum, and it's never too late to start.

If your hope has remained too vague, consider three practical ways you can take steps toward it today. Remember to include God's wisdom as you do, not creating shortcuts that will not work out in the end. There is always a way to follow God's nature and path of love and still move toward hope with integrity.

Daily Direction

Let the morning bring me word of your unfailing love,
for I have put my trust in you.
Show me the way I should go,
for to you I entrust my life.

PSALM 143:8 NIV

As we wake to each new day, our hearts can look with expectant hope to how God's mercy will meet us. When we are purposeful with turning our attention to the Lord each morning, it is an opportunity to set our intentions for the day. Quite like tuning into a radio station, as we set our hearts on God, we tune our spiritual ears to listen for the Lord.

God is a gracious guide. When we need direction, his wisdom directs us the way we should go. Much in the same way, when hope is at the forefront of our minds, we can more easily choose what to put our efforts toward and what to say no to. As we set our hearts on the hope before us, the steps to get there will light up as we make movement.

Make it a habit to ask the Lord to light the path before you as you make your choices today. Don't hesitate to look at the hopes you have and to see what aligns, while also relying on the Spirit's leading.

Bold as a Lion

We may boldly say: "The Lord is my helper; I will not fear.
What can man do to me?"

HEBREWS 13:6 NKJV

When we walk in the confidence of God with us, we can boldly approach whatever may come our way. God promises to never leave or forsake us. That is where our boldness comes from!

Our hopes are not based solely in what we can accomplish, but what God can do in and through us. He graciously helps us whenever we ask for it. Even more than this, he provides what we do not even know to ask for. God is powerful to save, and he does not how to fear. We can courageously walk through the terrain of this life knowing he is our guide and our constant friend.

Your hope is only as strong as your belief, and your confidence grows in the strength of secure relationships. Whenever you feel a bit overwhelmed by a task ahead of you, remember today's verse and walk boldly into it with the confidence of God's presence with you.

Peaceful Reliance

You, Lord, give true peace to those who depend on you, because they trust you. So, trust the Lord always, because he is our Rock forever.

ISAIAH 26:3-4 NCV

Trust is a key element of successful relationships. To have and maintain hope in our connection with others, trust is necessary. If we don't trust the people around us, or we don't think that it's possible to build that trust over time, what hope is there for meaningful relationship?

In Christ, we have the peace of God that transcends all understanding to guard our hearts and minds. This peace is pervasive and true, stemming from the faithful creator and sustainer of the universe. When we depend on the Lord, relying on him for all that we need, we experience the peace of his faithfulness and the power of his presence with us. He will always be a firm foundation to those who set their hopes on him.

If you want more palpable peace in your life, make sure your trust is in reliable and secure people and places. Above all, root your trust in the one who promises to never leave or forsake you.

Fully Convinced

He never stopped believing God's promise, for he was made strong in his faith to father a child. And because he was mighty in faith and convinced that God had all the power needed to fulfill his promises, Abraham glorified God!

ROMANS 4:20-21 TPT

Abraham could not choose when God's promise of a son would happen in his life. All he could do was what was possible and then trust and believe God. There are some hopes we have that we can't make happen. We can take steps toward them, but sometimes we reach the end of those and find that the rest is out of our control. In these times, faith is what will keep our hearts afloat in hope.

God is faithful and true. He fulfills his promises. If there are hopes we have that we can't do anything more than what we're already doing to see them come to life, then it's time to rest in faith. As we keep on believing, we don't stop living. There is so much more to our lives than that one hope. Let's trust God in his faithfulness and keep choosing love and movement in other areas.

If you need a boost of hope for a long-awaited promise, read through Hebrews 11. Faith is active, but it also takes the control out of your hands and puts your confidence in God who can do what you cannot.

Empowered in Generosity

Do not withhold good from those to whom it is due, when it is in your power to do it.

PROVERBS 3:27 ESV

Generosity is a virtue that God expresses through his character. He is gracious in all he does, not withholding good from those who look to him. We honor him when we choose to act in the same manner. Generosity may not always come naturally to us, but it is something we can grow in. When we choose to be gracious with our resources and our love, we benefit from it, too. Research shows that generosity is linked to feelings of satisfaction and happiness. Therefore, when we do good to others, we directly impact our own wellbeing.

Even small acts of generosity can have an impact on our hope. Shared hope is a powerful force, and when we meet needs that help others, it can serve to bolster their hope, as well as our own.

When you see a need that you can meet today, do the generous thing, and meet it. No act of generosity is too small, and it can go beyond giving money (though that counts, as well).

Grace to Serve

Just as each one has received a gift, use it to serve others,
as good stewards of the varied grace of God.

1 PETER 4:10 CSB .

If we only use our gifts and talents to benefit ourselves, we
miss out on the power of service. Stewardship is an important
element of taking responsibility for our impact in our roles and
in our communities. Every single one of us has a gift that we
can share with others. The things that often come easy to us,
or the gifts that we have cultivated with energy and skill can
be used to help others. This all works best when we serve one
another in love; no one person is left to do all the work alone.

Grace empowers us to choose love, even when it does not
come naturally. Service may not be the way we think to show
our care for someone, but its impact will be felt, regardless.
Let's not neglect the gift of grace that motivates us to serve
others

*Be intentional about serving others today, even if it is not in a
way that feels as if it is your gifting. Washing the dishes is as
powerful an act of service as speaking to crowds of people.*

Blessed in Giving

"I have been a constant example of how you can help those in need by working hard. You should remember the words of the Lord Jesus: 'It is more blessed to give than to receive.'"

ACTS 20:35 NLT

It is nice to receive a gift, but there is deep satisfaction in giving one thoughtfully. Paul ministered to many churches, but he always tried to be a blessing and not a burden. When he had to, he worked hard to not only meet his own needs, but to also cover the needs of those who served with him. He didn't count himself as above doing the work that was necessary to do!

As we remain humble in our own hearts and lives, we too can focus on what we can do to meet the needs of those around us. There is tremendous satisfaction in knowing our contributions matter. This, out of the overflow of God's fullness, is our source. There is so much grace to do the work. There is so much grace to serve in hope!

All that you do today, work at it as if you are working for the Lord, himself. And when you struggle, receive the plentiful grace of God from the fullness of his presence.

Direct Your Trust

When I am afraid,
I will put my trust in You.

PSALM 56:3 NASB

Fear is a natural reaction to a threat. It isn't a fault to feel it. However, when we are afraid, we can choose what we will do with that fear. There are sometimes when anxiety may take over our nervous systems. If we find ourselves overcome with fear, we can choose to direct our hearts in trust to what is true, faithful, and loving. Grounding ourselves in the moment through mindful breathing and by noting what is physically around us are tools that can help our nervous systems to calm

Directing our attention and directing the hope of our hearts toward the Lord can bring peace as we remember that he is powerful. He is present. He is capable. Though we may face unknowns, God is not afraid. Fear may cause us to hesitate, but courage will keep us moving in trust through it. When we are afraid, we don't have to rush to act in any way possible; we can slow down in the moment and direct our trust to the Lord.

When you feel afraid, your instincts may kick in. After you realize your fear, then you have a choice. Will you allow it to take over or will you do what you know to do to calm it? If that doesn't work, will you choose to trust God anyway?

Pour It Out

Cast all your anxiety on him
because he cares for you.

1 PETER 5:7 NIV

When anxiety remains sheltered in our bodies, we may find that stress affects us, not only emotionally, but also physically. Anxiety can negatively affect our cognitive function, gut health, and relationships. Toxic stress can create all sorts of difficulties for those who don't have tools or supports to deal with it.

God knows this about us! He doesn't just invite us to give him some of our cares and then carry the burden of worrying about other things. He knows what constant anxiety does to our whole beings, and he wants us to live wholly free and alive in his love. With this in mind, we can give him all our worries, our stress, and leave them there with him. He can handle what we don't know how to handle on our own. Pour out your heart to him and trust him to help you. Then, incredibly, you will find there is more space to focus on what he offers—love, joy, and so much hope.

Give every worry, question, and anxiety to the Lord. As soon as they come up, take them to him in prayer. Keep giving them to him until you realize that they are left with him and receive the peace and hope he offers.

Relentless Love

Height nor depth, nor any other created thing,
shall be able to separate us from the love of God
which is in Christ Jesus our Lord.

ROMANS 8:39 NKJV

The love of God weaves through our lives. Even through our trials and our greatest struggles, God's love is still present. Nothing can separate us from the mercy-kindness of God. Not the highest heights or deepest depths. Not anything created in this earth, not even the fiercest weapons, can keep us from the love of Christ.

What comfort there is in knowing that we cannot escape God's love! When we experience comfort, our hope, too, may grow. The comfort of God's presence reminds us that we are never alone in our grief. Even in pain of our own making, God's love is relentlessly close. Every moment is meaningful when we open our hearts to the Lord and let his love wash over us.

Lean into the love of God throughout your day, even when you are struggling to keep your emotions in check. His love is near, and he offers you renewal whenever you turn to him.

Seeds of Faith

"Because your faith is too small. I tell you the truth, if your faith is as big as a mustard seed, you can say to this mountain, 'Move from here to there,' and it will move. All things will be possible for you."

MATTHEW 17:20 NCV

A mustard seed is tiny, counting itself among the smallest seeds on the planet. Yet, it can grow into a large tree. We don't need a lot of faith, as Jesus revealed in Matthew 17; in fact, Jesus said that if we have the smallest amount, its power is strong enough to move mountains.

If we wait for bigger faith to take that first step toward hope, we may find ourselves wasting our whole lives, instead of using what little we have. When we wisely use what we have, we are trusted with more. If we truly want to see God's power at work in our lives, we must take the risk of putting our faith to the test.

Consider what you have faith for today, even if it seems like a small amount. Put that little bit of faith to work as you step out toward hope in a practical way.

Sustained by Hope

In all of my affliction I find great comfort in your promises,
for they have kept me alive!

PSALM 119:50 TPT

Hope can sustain us in the harshest climates and through the toughest of times. Hope keeps us tethered to the possibility of transformation and the promise of goodness. When our hearts are buoyed in hope, we inherently are motivated to move toward that goal.

It is so important that we feel seen and known in our troubles, too. Knowing that we are not the only one who struggles can bring relief and resolve to keep going. There are resources and tools available. There is support that can help us. Having a network of support can make all the difference for our hope. The promises of God are nothing to brush off, either. They can be just the courage our heart needs to press on in hope. God remains faithful, and his loyal love will not fail.

Write down one to three key promises or values that you want to direct this season of your life. Think of them as your anchors. Place them in prominent places where you will see them often, letting them serve as reminders of what your anchors of hope are.

Don't Forget

"There will never cease to be poor in the land. Therefore I command you, 'You shall open wide your hand to your brother, to the needy and to the poor, in your land.'"

DEUTERONOMY 15:11 ESV

Our hopes do not live in a vacuum. They are as present in our connections and relationships as they are when we are alone. Some of our greatest hopes may rely on the power of relationship. We do well to build our hope through community. We cannot turn a blind eye to the needy around us and remain in the love of Christ. If we are concerned about our own needs, we should also be concerned with the needs of those around us.

This isn't to say that we are responsible to fill every need. That's impossible! But every act of generosity matters. For those of us who know what it is to wait in hope for help, we should especially move in compassion readily and with generosity. The kingdom of Christ is exemplified through our love, not the least of which is shown to the poor and needy.

Is there a way that you actively engage in service or generosity with the poor or needy in your community? If not, consider what you can do. There are many organizations that you can volunteer your time or give donations to, but don't overlook your actual neighbors that are in need!

Resurrection Life

"I am the resurrection and the life.
The one who believes in me, even if he dies, will live."

JOHN 11:25 CSB

Our hope doesn't have to end with our mortal bodies. Though we may hold many hopes that we work toward in this life, there is still even more hope to hold onto—the hope of eternal life in the kingdom of Christ.

When Jesus told the Martha that he is the resurrection and the life, it was long before he gave his life and rose from the dead. But the truth remained: Jesus had the power to raise the dead to life, which he did shortly after by calling Lazarus out of his tomb. Martha was grieved by the loss of her brother, but Jesus offered her hope in the truth of who he was. He encouraged her, even while he felt his own grief. Let's not neglect the power of God's truth and nature to give us hope for every painful circumstance. Even if we die, in Christ we will live.

You don't have to ignore the realities of your circumstances or pretend to not be upset about them. Even there, you can come to Christ wholeheartedly, and he lovingly receives you and refreshes you in hope. Go to God with all your pain and your questions. He can handle them. Then listen for his reply.

Pleasant Places

The land you have given me is a pleasant land.
What a wonderful inheritance!

PSALM 16:6 NLT

When God is our Father, we inherit from the bounty of his kingdom. David's hope was in God. The fullness of his inheritance was in the relationship he had with him.

God is good, and he offers good things to his children. He puts us in pleasant places, giving refreshment to our souls. This does not mean that we will escape the challenges of life or times of need. But every blessing is a glimpse of his goodness. When we find ourselves in these pleasant places, let us give thanks to the Lord. When we find our hopes fulfilled, let us offer our joyous gratitude to God.

Identify one pleasant place in your current life. Be intentional in your gratitude today, treasuring the gift that it is.

Hopeful Blessing

"The Lord bless you, and keep you;
The Lord cause His face to shine on you,
And be gracious to you;
The Lord lift up His face to you,
And give you peace."

NUMBERS 6:24-26 NASB

When we put out our hopes for others, it does not have to be full of specifics. It is more than enough to want the best for them: to pray for the Lord's blessing over their lives. We cannot tell how the details of our lives, let alone anyone else's, will play out. It is much better to pray God's grace, presence, and peace over the people around us because those are accessible, no matter the season of life they find themselves in.

Let us be people who speak encouragement and hope to others. Let us wish God's best for them. Even if they are people we struggle to get along with, we can choose to pray the Lord's blessing over them. No matter who they are, they need grace, love, and peace.

Bless everyone you encounter today, even just between you and God. Even if it remains a simple "Lord, bless them." Let blessing be your gift when you're pleased and when you're frustrated!

Freedom's Invitation

The Lord is the Spirit,
and where the Spirit of the Lord is,
there is freedom.

2 CORINTHIANS 3:17 NIV

Where the Spirit of the Lord is, there is freedom. What do you need freedom from today? Are there areas of your life that you feel stuck or completely out of sorts? The Spirit of the Lord brings hope, direction, and liberty in God's love. There are always solutions for our problems in the wisdom of the Lord.

Knowing that we cannot outrun the Spirit of God should bring us even more hope in him when we realize that where the Spirit of the Lord is, there is freedom. There is freedom here and now for you!

Put your hope in God, and he will show you how to partner with his ways and how to walk in the freedom that he freely offers. Declare his freedom over your circumstances, especially the ones where you feel stuck in harmful cycles.

Waiting

"And now, LORD, what do I wait for?
My hope is in You."

PSALM 39:7 NKJV

There are times in life when we must wait; that is sure. But sometimes we hold ourselves back from taking the step we know to take. God won't push us in a direction we're unwilling to go. He won't do for us what he asks us to do. He partners with our faith, and he guides us and provides for us along the way.

Hope isn't just a wish for something to appear out of thin air. It is not a disconnected dream. Hope motivates us to pursue what we long for. It is belief and desire that work together toward an end. When our hope is in the Lord, in who he is and all that he promises, it will not disappoint. Let's press on and take that step we've been hesitating on.

If there is a specific area that you need to act in to move in the direction you want to go, do it today. Take that one small step. Keep doing that consistently, and you will find that the journey is made by taking each step forward!

Strong Roots

The person who trusts in the Lᴏʀᴅ will be blessed. The Lᴏʀᴅ will show him that he can be trusted. He will be strong, like a tree planted near water that sends its roots by a stream. It is not afraid when the days are hot; its leaves are always green. It does not worry in a year when no rain comes; it always produces fruit.

Jᴇʀᴇᴍɪᴀʜ 17:7-8 ɴᴄᴠ

When we trust our lives with the Lord, we are like trees planted by living waters. Even when the seasons shift and change, our source is close and nourishing. Trusting the Lord is the wisest thing we could do! It takes the pressure off of us and puts our hope in the greatness and goodness of God.

We need to be aware of the sources we draw nourishment from. Where do we put our hope and our trust? If our hopes only go as far as what the world offers, we will not be satisfied.

Root your trust in the Lord by remembering who he is. Let go of what you cannot control and focus on what you can do. Trust God with the rest!

Daily Commitment

Before you do anything,
put your trust totally in God
and not in yourself.
Then every plan you make will succeed.

PROVERBS 16:3 TPT

It is good practice to commit our time, our work, and our hearts to God every day. Sometimes, the mere act of intentionally putting our trust in God gives us the motivation we need to follow through with commitment on what is ahead of us to do. We put our trust in God, and we do the work. Success is in the follow through.

If we want to succeed, daily commitment is necessary. We must consistently do the work. As we pair our trust in God with the hope we have, we can see the necessary steps to take for each day, week, and month. Consistent effort will make a difference. Small steps will take us far if we keep taking them day by day. Hope doesn't disappoint, but it also doesn't leave things up to chance.

Before you begin your work each day, commit it to the Lord. Put your trust in him for all that you can't account for now and do the work that is in front of you to do. Wisdom will meet you as you lean on God's guidance and consistently take the steps in front of you.

Clean Slate

Let us draw near with a true heart in full assurance of faith,
with our hearts sprinkled clean from an evil conscience
and our bodies washed with pure water. Let us hold fast
the confession of our hope without wavering, for he who
promised is faithful.

HEBREWS 10:22-23 ESV

When we are weighed down by guilt, it can be hard to move
ahead in hope. Though we may try to fix our eyes on what
lies ahead, guilt is a heavy burden that slows our progress.
In Christ, we have full forgiveness of our sins. We can come
before him with all of our shame, pain, and mistakes, and
humble ourselves in his presence. He offers us the freedom of
his forgiveness and washes the guilt from our conscience. His
mercy is powerful enough to purify and redeem us!

It is so important to get our hearts right with God, and it is
also imperative that we do what is necessary to make things
right with the people we have wronged. We shouldn't ignore
the impact of our actions. Rather, when we take responsibility
and repent, we humble ourselves before others. We do what
we can to seek restoration and move ahead in hope.

*If you carry guilt about an area of your life, take it to the Lord.
Ask him to forgive you and empower you in his grace. If there
is someone you need to ask forgiveness from, do that as well.
There is hope for a new start in Christ.*

Worth It

How happy is anyone who has put his trust in the LORD
and has not turned to the proud
or to those who run after lies!

PSALM 40:4 CSB

Having trustworthy people in our lives doesn't only make our relationships stronger and our confidence greater, it acts as a support that allows for higher levels of hope, too. When we can depend on support being there when we need it, it is an incredible relief. It frees us up to focus on the areas that require our attention.

It is worth it to put our hope in God. What feels like a leap of faith turns into a benefit that leads to our joy as the Lord follows through in faithfulness. It is worth it to choose the ways of his wisdom, too. They are keys for life, leading us into integrity without any reason to hide or fear. When we build our lives on the truth instead of running after lies, we build on the solid rock of God's kingdom.

Whatever your hope today, follow through with the wisdom of God's ways. Be kind, tell the truth, and take responsibility. As you do, you will dwell in the rich freedom of God's love.

Transformative Power

Once you had no identity as a people;
now you are God's people.
Once you received no mercy;
now you have received God's mercy.

1 PETER 2:10 NLT

We all have a "before" time in our lives. Before we knew better, before the diagnoses, before kids, etc. Whatever the most significant dividing lines in our lives, we can be sure that God is faithful in mercy and relentless in power. No matter the challenges we face, we find ourselves in the "after" of being called children of God. He is our father, and he is overflowing with love for us.

There is incredible power in the mercy of God: mercy that transforms us, and love that revives us. In the heart of God, there are plans to give us a hope and a future (Jeremiah 29:11). If we want to experience the life-changing power of God at work in our hearts and lives, we have only to yield to God's love and allow it to direct us in hope. There is so much possibility for change!

Whether you find yourself in need of a new plan at this point in your life, or you simply have the desire for change in a certain area, there is mercy to drench your heart, your imagination, and your life. If there is hope, there is possibility for transformation.

Keep On Keeping On

Let endurance have its perfect result,
so that you may be perfect and complete,
lacking in nothing.

JAMES 1:4 NASB

Though our patience and endurance may be tested, it is the choice to keep persisting in hope that will make all the difference. We may not choose our hardships, but we can choose how we react to and move through them.

Resilience in hardship can help us to shape into more loving, patient, and understanding people. As we endure the challenges of life with open hearts, we grow in grace. Having hope can help us to stay motivated to keep going, even when times are hard. The refining processes of life all happen under pressure. The fires of testing don't make us weaker; they make us who we are. If we need an encouragement to keep going, let us remember that every trial is an opportunity for God's mercy to meet us in it.

What helps you endure hard times? Think of three tools that you know can help you keep going when you're tempted to give up, and remember rest is a valid option!

Living by Faith

Every good and perfect gift is from above, coming down from the Father of the heavenly lights, who does not change like shifting shadows.

ROMANS 1:17 NIV

God's character is unchangeable. His nature will never diminish or shift. He is always faithful, always true, always loving, and always righteous. He is the firm foundation of our faith. We may not know how the details of how our lives will play out, but we can have confidence in the steadfast presence of the Lord, who is clothed in light.

As we taste and see the goodness of God through the gifts that bring peace, joy, expectation, and love, our very faith and hope are nourished and strengthened. Every good gift is evidence of a good God. As our confidence grows in the faithfulness of God, so do our expectations of his goodness. There is always hope when we realize we cannot escape the overwhelming love of our God through the gifts of his grace.

Write down every good gift (every good thing!) in your life. As you go through them, thank God for the gifts of his goodness.

Living to Please

Do I now persuade men, or God? Or do I seek to
please men? For if I still pleased men, I would not be a
bondservant of Christ.

GALATIANS 1:10 NKJV

If we seek to please our parents and their ideas of what is best
for us, we will make decisions that take us in that direction.
If we want to make our friends proud, we may choose to do
what matters to them. When we live to impress or satisfy
others, we may find our lives being spent on things that we
find don't matter to us in the end. To live in authenticity, we
can take the wisdom of others into account while also taking
ownership of our own decisions.

God's ways are perfect. They are righteous. They are for our
good. When we live to please him, we will also find freedom in
the integrity of his love. Pleasing God is much more about how
we live than the jobs we take and the trajectory of our dreams.
He is with us through it all. When we live for the Lord, we
choose to prioritize his nature—being loving, kind, patient, and
generous—in every area of our lives. As we live authentically in
who we were created to be, we can please God in the way we
treat others.

*God has given you control over your choices. Do you feel
empowered to choose what pleases him in moving toward
your hopes?*

Hope for Renewal

If we confess our sins, he will forgive our sins, because we can trust God to do what is right. He will cleanse us from all the wrongs we have done.

1 JOHN 1:9 NCV

When we hide from others, we may find ourselves feeling unable to connect in a deep way. We were created to be fully seen and known: to be loved to life, even in our mistakes and failures. When we know we can be honest about how we are struggling and how we have wronged others, vulnerability has a place to be witnessed. We will always have to choose vulnerability, but when we do in safe relationships, trust is built.

We don't ever need to fear the reception we have in Christ. As we confess our sins to him, he cleanses us in mercy and encourages us in kindness. He is a safe landing place, no matter the mess we find ourselves in. Knowing we can bare our souls before him, hope has a place to grow, for there is always opportunity for a fresh start in his mercy.

If there is something that you have kept hidden, even from just discussing with another person, consider reaching out to a trusted friend. If nothing else, take it to the Lord in prayer, and ask for his wisdom, his help, and his covering.

More than Expected

"A thief has only one thing in mind—he wants to steal,
slaughter, and destroy. But I have come to give you
everything in abundance, more than you expect—
life in its fullness until you overflow!"

JOHN 10:10 TPT

How gracious Jesus is to us. This isn't true only when we
first come to him and receive his mercy for the first time. It is
always true. Every time we turn toward him in yielded humility,
God offers us more than we ask for, more than we expect. He
is always better than we imagine him to be.

Let's not limit God's goodness to our own understanding.
We taste his goodness and see glimpses of his glory, but
they are only glimmers. He is much more wonderful than we
know! Let's raise our expectations of the abundance of God
according to who Jesus says he is. He is always overflowing
in kindness; if we find ourselves lacking, we have only to drink
from his fountain of grace again. Every time we thirst, may
it signal us to go to the living waters of God's presence and
drink once more. He puts no limits on us, so let's take him at
his generous word.

Go to God with every need, every hope, and every signal of
hunger or thirst today. He is an overflowing source of love
that will enrich your soul, your heart, your mind, your body,
and your life!

Gentle and Easy

"Take my yoke upon you, and learn from me, for I am gentle and lowly in heart, and you will find rest for your souls. For my yoke is easy, and my burden is light."

MATTHEW 11:29-30 ESV

God is not a taskmaster who demands endless work from us. Too often he is portrayed as a disapproving authority figure and not like the tender father he is. He invites us to learn from him, and as we do, we discover that he is gentle, patient, and easy to please. He delights in us as we follow his ways. He doesn't expect perfection from us. He wants growth and trust.

Jesus invites us to lay down our heavy burdens with him. As he offers us his help, we find the load lightened by the strength of his frame. He doesn't ever require us to struggle our way through on our own strength. He always has grace to empower us. He offers rest for our souls whenever we need it. What a gentle and humble help he is!

If you are not careful, you can fall into the trap of thinking you can earn God's favor. Resisting that urge, take your burdens to the Lord and ask for his gentle peace to fill your soul with rest. You can find peace of mind and heart in him today.

September

Let us hold tightly without wavering
to the hope we affirm,
for God can be trusted
to keep his promise.

HEBREWS 10:23 NLT

Greater Trust

Some take pride in chariots, and others in horses,
but we take pride in the name of the LORD our God.

PSALM 20:7 CSB

When the powerful of this world use their influence to intimidate others, they are not reflecting the heart of God. God does not coerce us into his love. He doesn't demand our blind obedience. He invites us into a living relationship. When we bind our lives to the Living God, we don't depend on the promises of the systems of this world for our hope. We rely on God, who is strong to save in any and every season and circumstance.

Hope reaches into the possibilities of the future, goals for a greater good than we already know. Holding onto hope doesn't mean denying the beauty of what we now have. It gives us a path forward in purpose. We can be sure that as we trust in the name of the Lord our God, he makes a way for us, even where there seems to be none.

Instead of relying on your own resources today, ask God to give you greater vision for his power at work in your life. Take a step of faith in the direction he reveals, and trust that he will continue to guide and provide for you.

Mercy Matters

"Healthy people don't need a doctor—sick people do."
Then he added, "Now go and learn the meaning of this
Scripture: 'I want you to show mercy, not offer sacrifices.'
For I have come to call not those who think they are
righteous, but those who know they are sinners."

MATTHEW 9:12-13 NLT

We are lifelong learners. It takes practice to choose mercy,
and this also applies to hope. When our reserves are running
low, we may find choosing the loving thing is harder. But this
doesn't make it impossible. Having tools available to help us
reset, but to also choose the way we want to live, is important.

Setting goals and prioritizing what is truly important to us is
a keyway to make sure that we set ourselves up for success.
If we aren't proactive about it, we will not grow in mercy. If
we don't put ourselves in positions to practice kindness and
generosity, we may find our progress slow-going. With a bit of
proactive motivation, we can set ourselves up for building our
hope while following the ways of Christ with intention.

*Consider practical ways you want to grow in kindness and
generosity. Choose two to actively put into practice this week.*

Love in Action

Little children, let's not love with word or with tongue,
but in deed and truth.

1 John 3:18 NASB

If we don't do what we say we will do, the people in our lives won't be able to depend on us. Consistency and follow through build trust in our relationships. In the same way, if we talk a good talk about how much we love the Lord, but we are unkind to others, there is a severe disconnect between what we say we value and what we do.

Hope grows well in nourished soil. We nourish our relationships by building trust. Our character matters, and so does how we treat people. If we take seriously the call of Christ to love God and to love others the way we love ourselves, we make it a priority to show it through our actions. Let's love others by being people of our word and by extending kindness and generosity whenever we can.

Think about what you have promised or offered others. Choose one to act on today, and let it be an offering of love and also a reflection of your character to follow through.

Steadfast Hope

They will have no fear of bad news;
their hearts are steadfast, trusting in the LORD.

PSALM 112:7 NIV

The psalms are filled with God's people coming up against incredible odds and putting their hope in the Lord in it all. God can handle our anxieties and our greatest problems. He is a sure place to put our hope, for he never fails in faithful mercy to help those who call out to him.

Psalm 112:5 says, "Good will come to those who are generous and lend freely, who conduct their affairs with justice." The righteous, the next verse goes on, will not be shaken and will be remembered even after they are gone. These are whose hearts are secure; they are steadfast in trust and secure in hope. We can truly put our hope in God, even as we live in the way he has called us to.

Take your bad news, your worries, and your fears to God. Pour them out before him, and after you have, do the simple things you know to do.

Renewed Perspective

Be renewed in the spirit of your mind.

EPHESIANS 4:23 NKJV

Hope doesn't just offer us something to look forward to. It isn't only a goal to take steps toward. It certainly is more than just a wish for good. Hope transforms our perspective by renewing our mind in the possibility of God's goodness as it meets our lives. Hope is the belief that our future can be better than our past, and that we take an active part in making that future a reality.

If we want a different outcome than what we have previously experienced, we must choose a different pathway. We must be willing to see from a different perspective and to believe that it is achievable. Hope motivates us in creativity, even as we walk it out. Whether or not we consider ourselves creative, we are made in the image of the Creator. His creativity offers us the wisdom of his creative solutions, but we must be willing to try new things, to do things differently, and to believe that the risk of daring to be different is worth it.

Ask God for a new way to think about your problems. His creative problem solving can help you to create movement toward hope and to see things from an entirely different perspective. Try out a new technique and see if it helps!

Strength in Weakness

My body and my mind may become weak,
but God is my strength. He is mine forever.

PSALM 73:26 NCV

When we belong to God, he offers us the resources of his limitless power and love. He shares what is his with us. That is a beautiful reality to keep in mind. Even when our bodies give out and our minds weaken, God remains our strength. His power does not diminish, even when we do.

It is a beautiful thing to keep in mind that our lives are short. We don't know how long we have our health or our strength. Let's give gratitude for what we have while we have it, keeping in mind that every moment is a gift. We are not worth any less in our sickness, our struggles, or in our weakness. We are as beloved in those moments as we are on our strongest days. We can keep our lives in perspective while also leaning into the hope of God's love, his nearness, and his strength every season we go through!

Ask the Spirit to reveal the love of the Lord to you in a fresh and meaningful way today. Wait in his presence. Whether you feel completely ready to face the day or are struggling to do anything, the Lord's strength is near and his heart for you never wavers.

A Helping Hand

By helping each other with your troubles,
you truly obey the law of Christ.

GALATIANS 6:2 NCV

What does helping someone have to do with hope? Science is showing that the benefits of generosity are as real as we perceive them to be. Studies have shown that both giving and receiving money light up the same area of our brains, the striatum, where dopamine rewards activities that bring satisfaction. Even more, when we witness the positive impact of our service or gift, there is real joy released through serotonin and oxytocin into our bodies.

Obedience always has a reward. Obedience to Christ's law of love is good for us, not just for others. It benefits everyone. Our hope grows in connection with others. When we participate in and receive help when it is needed, we release grace for gratitude, but also for the hope of better days to come.

Don't resist helping when it is in your power to do so today. Small acts of kindness add up to a wealth of gratitude, joy, and hope, so don't hold back.

Infused with Strength

"I drew you to myself from the ends of the earth and called
you from its farthest corner. I say to you:
'You are my servant; I have chosen you. I have not rejected
you! Do not yield to fear, for I am always near.'"

ISAIAH 41:9-10 TPT

It is an incredible experience to be loved so well that we don't
doubt our worth. God chooses us, gathers us into his family,
and gives us the covering of his very name. When we are
covered by the power of the Lord, known as his very own, it
is important to remember whom we belong to. He is always
near, faithful to infuse us with strength and help us in every
situation.

Sometimes the hope and courage we need are as close as
remembering our identity in Christ. We need not be defined
by our past, and our futures are filled with hope in him. Let us
not forget who we are, and how completely we are loved by
the King of kings and Lord of lords. What hopeful strength is
ours as we remember this.

*Take some time to think about who you are to God and
who he says he is to you. Trust his faithfulness, and let his
character be your strength.*

Trust His Timing

Humble yourselves, therefore, under the mighty hand of God so that at the proper time he may exalt you, casting all your anxieties on him, because he cares for you.

1 PETER 5:6-7 ESV

Our timing is not the same as God's. Though we may want to rush toward a goal and see it happen as quickly as possible, there is wisdom in knowing that lasting impact requires patience and care along the way. When we are discouraged by our timelines running out, we can take hope in the truth that God continues to work, and so can we. Sometimes the work is waiting, and sometimes it is pushing forward. At all times, the work will be worth it, even as we remember that God can do far more than we can on our own.

This world loves a quick fix, but the truth is that most good things take time. Even when we receive what we want in the moment, the satisfaction doesn't last. We quickly move on to wanting the next thing. Let's make room for gratitude, remembering that God's timing is perfect, and it takes all things into account. As we nurture thankful hearts, we can remain humble in trusting that we will have all we need when we need it.

Make a gratitude list of what you are thankful for especially those things you once dreamed of having that you now do. God will continue to lead you and provide for you.

Hope in Our Homes

If anyone does not provide for his own family,
especially for his own household,
he has denied the faith
and is worse than an unbeliever.

I TIMOTHY 5:8 CSB

The importance of caring for others cannot be overstated. Love is a force that reaches out, first in our own homes and lives, and then it stretches outward from there. We cannot overlook the importance of caring and providing for our own. Our families and households must be our main priority. Ministry should never come before the health and wellbeing of those closest to us.

We may find that we need to get our priorities straight when it comes to our home lives. If we are living, there is hope for new patterns. We cannot control how others choose to live, but we can certainly take control over our own priorities and choices. Let's make sure they're aligned with what truly matters, adjusting where necessary.

Is there anything you've been ignoring in your home life that needs a fresh burst of hope followed by action? Ask the Lord to reveal where you need to reassess your priorities and the steps you can take to do just that.

Stay Sensitive

We who are strong must be considerate
of those who are sensitive about things like this.
We must not just please ourselves.

ROMANS 15:1 NLT

Cold hearts do not represent the heart of God. God doesn't
demean people for where they are; he meets them there with
kindness and grace. If we truly want to be like Christ, then
allowing our hearts to be sensitive to the plight of others is
paramount. Also taking care to not offend people on purpose
because they believe differently than we do is a kind and
gracious act of care.

The sensitive are not the weak ones of the world, not really.
Not in the kingdom of Christ. The sensitive ones are those
that allow compassion to lead them, to change their minds
and their approach when they see how they have harmed
others. They are those who are willing to admit when they are
wrong, to love others they disagree with simply because it is
the loving thing to do, and who consider the impact of their
actions. Hope is released through them and in them as they
remain strong in character and purposeful in their service to
others.

*Reflect on your thoughts about what it means to be sensitive
in this world. How can you be sensitive for Christ and his
kingdom?*

Life Persists

We are afflicted in every way, but not crushed; perplexed,
but not despairing; persecuted, but not abandoned; struck
down, but not destroyed; always carrying around in the
body the dying of Jesus, so that the life of Jesus may also
be revealed in our body.

2 CORINTHIANS 4:8-10 NASB

The life of Christ persists in our lives as we persevere in hope
through every trial. We don't have to give into despair when
the going gets tough. In fact, when the pressures of life are
building, it is the right time to keep our hearts set on the one
who relieves our worries and who strengthens us in weakness.

The resurrection power of Christ is our hope, no matter the
struggles we go through. If our hope is in the ease with which
we can live, we will find it buckles under the first sign of
trouble. God never promised us easy lives if we follow him.
But he did promise us his pervasive peace, no matter what we
experience. He promised that his presence would go with us.
He promised that we will one day be relieved from every pain,
yes, but that even as we heal and persevere in this life, there is
a rich reward in knowing and following him.

*Set up a reminder or a verse that you can turn to when you
are discouraged by unexpected troubles or frustrations. You
can redirect your heart and mind in hope as you do.*

Stronghold of Hope

"Return to your fortress, you prisoners of hope; even now
I announce that I will restore twice as much to you."

ZECHARIAH 9:12 NIV

No matter what has bound us in the past, God offers us
freedom in his love. He calls us to come back to him, to return
to the fortress of his kingdom and to find hope in him. He will
restore what life has taken from us, and he will give us even
more than what we started out with. He really is that gracious
and good.

Don't let the discouragement of loss keep you from hoping
in him. God is not finished working miracles of mercy in
your life. He is the restorer, redeemer, and resurrection life.
Nothing is impossible for him. He creates gardens out of the
ashes of disappointment. He sows goodness into the lining
of our suffering. There is nothing he cannot renew, and this
includes you!

*Hope is a renewable resource. You cannot reach the end of
it. Go to the Lord with all that you carry and trust him to
do what he promises to. He is faithful and true, and he can
restore what you could never dream of repairing on your own.*

Still Praising

Why are you cast down, O my soul?
And why are you disquieted within me?
Hope in God; For I shall yet praise Him,
The help of my countenance and my God.

PSALM 42:11 NKJV

There is power in choosing to praise God in our troubles and in the face of overwhelming odds against us. He is faithful, he is trustworthy, and he is true. He won't ever change from being loyal to his word or meeting us whenever we turn to him. In fact, as soon as we shift our gaze, we find that he is closer than we could have realized. He is the God who never leaves or forsakes us, after all.

When our hearts are discouraged, we can still choose to praise God. When we are depressed, we can still choose to put our hope in him. As we remind our souls who he is, we direct our attention to the power of his name. He hasn't failed yet, and he won't today.

Choose to praise God, no matter what comes your way today. Pick a song to sing to him or play worship music in the background as you continue to direct your heart in hope.

Love Never Fails

Love never ends. There are gifts of prophecy, but they will be ended. There are gifts of speaking in different languages, but those gifts will stop. There is the gift of knowledge, but it will come to an end.

1 CORINTHIANS 13:8 NCV

There are many endings in this life, many beginnings, too. It can be hard to transition through the changes of life when endings can be so painful. But there is hope: hope for a fresh start, and hope in the fact that love is present through it all. Though marriages fail, loved ones die, and tragedies occur, love does not let up. It is constant: less like a thread and more like a rushing river that runs through the landscape of our lives.

If we truly believe this, that love never ends, than we can rest assured that no matter what we do if we do it in love; it matters. It resounds into eternity. Its impact remains. We may question how to live in a complicated world, but if we choose to err on the side of love, we align ourselves with the kingdom of God because *God is love*. Even if we aren't successful in many areas, if we are successful at loving others, that is all that matters.

Above all else today, choose love. In your interactions, in your attitudes, and in your work. Choose love because it never fails.

Heart Desires

> May Yahweh give you every desire of your heart
> and carry out your every plan as you go to battle.
>
> PSALM 20:4 TPT

There is a difference between the desires of our heart and our hope, though they can certainly overlap. Desire is the strong feeling of wanting something. Hope is the expectation that something that we wish for can happen. When our heart desires something, it can cause us to move ahead in action toward the hope we have.

Without hope, we may never do anything with the impulse of desire. It is natural to want things, but getting clear about what we really want it is especially important. As we move ahead in action, connecting belief with desire, it sets us on a path forward. Let's be sure to be intentional about which paths we take by checking in on our desires and our objectives.

Plans are a necessary part of hope. When you have desire for something and the vision to see it happen, you can take each step as you see it. Pick a desire you have and plan to move ahead in hope this week.

Inner Confidence

I have been crucified with Christ. It is no longer I who live, but Christ who lives in me. And the life I now live in the flesh I live by faith in the Son of God, who loved me and gave himself for me.

GALATIANS 2:20 ESV

When we yield our lives to Christ, his love transforms our motivations. He makes us new in him. It is not that we lose ourselves in him, but that we come fully alive in him. He breaks the bondage of our sin, allowing us to see more clearly and showing us the path to his kingdom: one paved in mercy, peace, and hope.

We are still fully us with all our unique personality traits and gifts. Under Christ's leadership, we can grow in confidence and use what he has given us for the greater good. Christ's presence empowers us to choose kindness, to choose lifegiving encouragement, and to choose love, even when it is the unpopular route to take. He is our confidence, not pleasing others. When we live to please God, we can take courageous steps of hope, whether we're alone or with others.

Ask the Lord for direction throughout your day and follow the Spirit's lead. Remember that how you live (your nature, how you treat others, choosing integrity, etc.) is more important than the details of what you do.

Born Again

To all who did receive him, he gave them the right to be children of God, to those who believe in his name, who were born, not of natural descent, or of the will of the flesh, or of the will of man, but of God.

JOHN 1:12-13 CSB

Though we are all born of the flesh, born into this world and into families that we don't choose, there is a greater family we can join. However familiar we are with the term "born again," Jesus lays out its meaning for us. In John 3:5,7 Jesus says, "unless someone is born of water and the Spirit, he cannot enter the kingdom of God... he must be born again."

Jesus spent much of his ministry baptizing those who came to him in faith. There is incredible power in the symbolism of rising from the water a new person, joining the family of God with our willingness and witness. It is a marker to commemorate our dedication. Let's not neglect the power of uniting our lives with God in this way, for we have been given the right to be called children of God. If we are, let's unashamedly proclaim it with baptism and rise, with hope, in Christ.

Have you been baptized? If you have, look back on that time and consider the power of your commitment. If you haven't, what has kept you from doing it?

Power of Belonging

You Gentiles are no longer strangers and foreigners.
You are citizens along with all of God's holy people.
You are members of God's family.

EPHESIANS 2:19 NLT

In the kingdom of God, there are no foreigners or strangers.
There are no borders or barriers between us. We must be
careful, then, when we divide ourselves from others where God
has already broken down the walls between us. Let us join with
God's heart and be builders of bridges instead of walls.

There is incredible power and hope in knowing that we
belong. Wherever we have felt at home is a powerful indicator
of belonging. We don't have to agree, assimilate, or shape shift
to truly belong. Each of us is welcomed in the Lord just as we
are. He loves us to life where we are at, and he delights in our
differences. Can we do the same in our communities? Studies
show that diverse and inclusive spaces earn greater trust and
commitment from their members. There is hope for continued
change and community strengthening as we choose to treat
each other with love, honor, and respect.

*If the spaces you are in are not diverse, consider how you can
intentionally broaden the demographic of people you interact
with. It will help you understand others better, and to get a
glimpse of God's heart for those who are different than you.*

Eternity in View

While we look not at the things which are seen, but at the things which are not seen; for the things which are seen are temporal, but the things which are not seen are eternal.

2 CORINTHIANS 4:18 NASB

If all we ever focus our attention on is what is right in front of us, we miss out on the wisdom of shifting our perspective. We need both; we need the bigger vision along with the ability to be engaged in the present. Faith requires looking beyond what we can now see, and hope allows us to take hold of it by looking at the possibilities there.

Action and belief go together as we reach into the eternal truth of God's kingdom and allow our understanding to transform as we walk our faith out in practical ways. Anyone who's ever had a dream and worked toward it knows this balance. The beautiful thing about partnering with God is that we do our part, but we don't rely on that work alone to realize the benefits of what we hope for. We can shift our perspective to God's wonderful nature when the going gets tough. He helps us, and he will continue to even until the end of the age.

Take time to ask God to show you his higher perspective of your life. Ask him for insight to keep moving in the direction of your hope. He is good, and he is faithful, and he will help you.

Higher Wavelength

Since, then, you have been raised with Christ,
set your hearts on things above, where Christ is, seated at
the right hand of God. Set your minds on things above,
not on earthly things.

COLOSSIANS 3:1-2 NIV

It is possible to harness hope and use it as a tool for achieving positive mental health outcomes. Though it is not a cure-all approach, it can significantly improve our perspectives, which can lead to higher resilience and help us to get positive outcomes by shaping our behavior. Hope can shift our expectations of the future.

There are many factors that can influence the level of our hope. Whether or not we have a supportive community, places where we feel seen, and access to tools that can help us problem solve are all elements that can make a tremendous difference to our hope. Simply redirecting our expectations can also make a difference. When we set our hearts on things above, we join with the perspective of Christ where all things are possible, and no problem is too big to solve. What a beautiful and important starting place.

Consider the level of hope you have today. Find a supportive space or person to be present in, and allow yourself to borrow hope from others, if that's where you are today.

Promised Protection

He saves the needy from the sword,
From the mouth of the mighty,
And from their hand.
So the poor have hope,
And injustice shuts her mouth.

JOB 5:15-16 NKJV

It is a sad reality that the poor are always with us, not because there is something wrong with them, but because the reality remains that poverty is a struggle consistent through time. If we want to sow hope into this world and into our communities, a perfect place to do that is through helping those struggling to get by.

God promises to protect the vulnerable, so why would we resist that impulse? There are many in this world that are vulnerable and without resources to help them. It is important that we don't relegate different demographics to certain statuses, and our help doesn't only go to those we deem worthy. In God's eyes, all are his. All are welcome. All deserve the protection and dignity of being seen in their humanity. Hope grows through kindness, compassion, and through breaking barriers. Let's be harbingers of hope in our own communities!

Do one thing that practically helps someone in need today. No act of kindness or service is insignificant.

Living Hope

Christ was chosen before the world was made, but he was shown to the world in these last times for your sake. Through Christ you believe in God, who raised Christ from the dead and gave him glory. So your faith and your hope are in God.

1 PETER 1:20-21 NCV

It is important that we have our hope and faith in something larger than ourselves, but where do we direct that belief? Is it to the world and its systems? Though we can work for a better society, systems are imperfect. They are not able to serve all in the same manner. This doesn't mean we shouldn't try to make a difference, but our greatest hope isn't in this world at all. It is in the Creator who formed it, and all of us, into existence.

Jesus is our living hope. He reminds us of his constant presence with us, his never-ending love, and insistent grace that empowers us in our weakness. When we live with love as our covering and motivation, and we work for a better future for all, we live from and for hope.

Knowing that with Christ all things are possible for those who believe, put hope into action by taking a practical step of faith today.

Keep in Mind

Don't owe anything to anyone, except your outstanding debt to continually love one another, for the one who learns to love has fulfilled every requirement of the law.

ROMANS 13:8 TPT

While feeling the pull of our debt to others is uncomfortable, it needn't be. We can work to pay off our debt and allow room for love to motivate us to action in other ways. When we are in the habit of transactional living, it can be tough to break out of it. We cannot avoid the responsibility we have to pay our taxes, bills, and other necessities, but this should not consume our focus. These are givens, but love motivates us to be generous in the ways that we can without expecting anything in return.

Even if we take money out of the mix, how we spend our time is just as important. We cannot escape the law of love that Jesus laid out for all those who follow him. He teaches that love covers all the other commandments. It really is not too simple to say that if we make our choices in the light of loving (honoring) God and others, our lives will be pleasing to God.

Don't avoid your responsibilities today and look for ways outside of them to let love motivate you in kindness toward others.

Liberating Truth

"You will know the truth,
and the truth will set you free."

JOHN 8:32 ESV

Jesus explained that true freedom is one that begins in our souls. When our hearts, minds, and understanding are liberated, we can walk in the clarity Christ's light brings to our lives. We do this by embracing all that he teaches and adopting his ways as our own. In Christ, we are set free. In freedom, we can walk in the hope of his love every day of our lives.

When we are not bogged down by the heavy yoke of confusion or competing interests, we are freed up to live with purpose and intention. In the truth of Christ, we find a path and the grace to imperfectly walk it. God himself is our guide and our strength. His presence is our hope and our protection. We need never fear, for his love is constant and he leads us on the path of healing and restoration for freedom's sake.

Where you are trapped in fear, God wants to set you free. Take hold of his truth and his presence with you. Ask for the grace to believe and follow him and walk into your freedom!

Use It Well

Submit as free people, not using your freedom as a cover-up for evil, but as God's slaves. Honor everyone. Love the brothers and sisters. Fear God. Honor the emperor.

1 PETER 2:16-17 CSB

Freedom in Christ doesn't come with stipulations. And still, his law of love remains. We are as free as can be, but that doesn't mean that there is not a better way to follow than our own whims. The love of Christ compels us to live honorable lives of integrity. That we would honor everyone (no exceptions), that we would love our brothers and sisters in Christ, and that we would live with all respect due to our Father. Love also calls us to honor our leaders. Love is not an excuse to do whatever we want; it considers others as highly as we consider ourselves.

Therefore, we should use the freedom we have well. Choosing what aligns with God's kingdom, and not the kingdoms of this earth. God's ways are always better. His love really is more extravagant than we allow for. Let's practice generosity of heart as much as we do generosity with our resources, honoring others always.

Make a concerted effort to honor everyone around you today.

Liberated Expectations

Because you belong to him, the power of the life-giving Spirit
has freed you from the power of sin that leads to death.

ROMANS 8:2 NLT

Belonging to Christ means that not only do we have freedom
in him, but we have freedom of hope! We know that there is
far more that God can and will do than we could ever think
to ask him. As we submit our hearts to his love, he transforms
them in his nature. As we journey this life with him as our
guide, we discover repeatedly how merciful, how faithful, and
how true he really is.

No matter the deaths we have faced, the losses we have
endured, or the challenges that have come our way, there
is always the promise of goodness in the redemptive power
of Christ. His mercies are new every morning. His love sows
expectation in our hearts as we experience it in a myriad of
miraculous ways in our right-now lives. Let's not limit our
hopes to what tomorrow may bring, but to the incredible
faithfulness of God who is with us no matter what.

*No matter how your day started, the hope of Christ's love is
with you. Ask him to strengthen your hope as you choose to
press into him throughout your day.*

Extravagant Grace

By grace you have been saved through faith;
and this is not of yourselves, it is the gift of God.

EPHESIANS 2:8 NASB

Grace cannot be earned. It also cannot be controlled. We are saved by grace, and we are kept in Christ by grace. Grace is a gift, and it was designed this way so that no man or woman could take credit for what God alone could offer.

As we receive the grace of God, it meets us right where we are. We don't have to dress ourselves up or put on a façade. He sees us just as we are, and he rushes in to meet us, even in the middle of our messes. The power of grace is for all; it is not a gift offered some and refused others. It is gloriously free, and it is overwhelmingly good. Grace empowers us to hope for better days, for it is the strength of God meeting us in the reality of where we are. As we are strengthened and graciously seen, known, loved, and forgiven, we have room to hope where we might only have felt dread before. Praise God for the incredible gift of grace!

Receive the grace of God in the reality of your circumstances today. Allow the Spirit of God to meet you in your weakness, for he is powerful to save, to liberate, and to redeem.

Stuck in Place

"Have I not commanded you? Be strong and courageous.
Do not be afraid; do not be discouraged,
for the Lord your God will be with you wherever you go."

JOSHUA 1:9 NIV

Hope motivates us to move in action. It gives us both a goal to work toward, and the desire to get there. But what about when we second guess ourselves due to fear? That is where perspective, encouragement, and the power of connection can help us from staying stuck. God promises to be with us wherever we go. He is so gracious with us; he knows that we are prone to fear, but he does not want us to stay stuck there. He reminds us whenever we need it, that we can be strong and courageous because he goes with us.

If it weren't for the Lord's presence, we may have reason to fear. However, we have access to God's presence at all times and in all spaces. His Spirit does not leave us or forsake us. When fear has us questioning our next step, let's look at what exactly it is that we fear. If it lies in the unknown outcome, let's take God at his word that he will faithfully be with us and take that step of courage.

Hope has the power to get you unstuck. If you need a dash of courage, ask the Lord for the perspective of his presence with you in the unknowns you face.

Safe Place

The LORD is good,
A stronghold in the day of trouble;
And He knows those who trust in Him.

NAHUM 1:7 NKJV

Our nervous systems are not built to be in never-ending cycles of stress, but the truth is that many of us don't know how to live any differently. Studies show that toxic stress affects everything from cognitive function to generational trends. One of the simplest ways to infuse hope into people is to provide safe spaces where they feel connected, supported, and have the tools they need for help to get through. Only then can people (and families) begin to heal and know peace.

We all need safe spaces in our lives: places we know we can go to get away from the stresses of life, but also to find supports to get through them. Hope thrives in community. When we can show up as we are and receive tools, encouragement, and presence with us in the challenges, hope has a place to grow.

What are the places that you feel most secure? Who are the people that you feel you can be your truest self with? These are places and people to treasure; they are arbiters of hope in your life. Reach out and thank one or two of these people today.

October

Those who hope in the LORD
will renew their strength.
They will soar on wings like eagles;
they will run and not grow weary,
they will walk and not be faint.

ISAIAH 40:31 NIV

Real Peace

"I will give peace, real peace, to those far and near, and I will heal them," says the Lord.

ISAIAH 57:19 NCV

The power of God's peace is not just for those who have known it all their lives. In fact, the Lord made it clear that his real peace is for those both far and near. It is peace that heals, peace that saves, peace that restores the soul.

The peace of God transcends our earthly experiences. Even in war, we can know the overwhelming peace of God in our hearts and minds. His peace is pervasive. It doesn't leave us. It can shift the atmosphere of our homes and shift the trajectory of our hope. We are more able to dream when we dwell in peace and not in chaos or confusion. Let's embrace the peace of God that he offers to us today.

Where there is confusion, God's peace brings clarity. Where there is tension, it brings relief. Be a pursuer of peace in your relationships today. When you make choices, think of the portion of peace you offer others and yourself through them. Choose the peaceful, restful, restorative, hopeful path.

Called to Peace

Let your heart be always guided by the peace of the Anointed One, who called you to peace as part of his one body. And always be thankful.

COLOSSIANS 3:15 TPT

In Romans 12:18, Paul instructed, "Do your best to live as everybody's friend," or in other words, to live at peace with everyone. Jesus himself said that those who make peace will be recognized as true children of God (Matthew 5:9). There is no shortage of instruction in God's Word to be pursuers of peace.

Hope is given the opportunity to grow as we make peace a priority in our relationships, communities, and lifestyles. We should not try to push others' buttons for the fun of it. We shouldn't look to pick fights with those who have different viewpoints. We can be pursuers of peace and live in the integrity of truth at the same time.

Make peace a priority today. It's more important than being right.

Wise Instruction

Receive instruction in wise dealing,
in righteousness, justice, and equity.

PROVERBS 1:3 ESV

When we receive wisdom that brings clarity and discipline, we also receive wisdom that helps us to choose what is right, just, and fair. The wisdom of God's ways offers us direction to do the right thing in our relationships. It gives us clarity to choose the better path in moving toward hope. It is full of peace, truth, and justice.

When it comes to hope, wisdom can play a vital role. Wisdom gives us the vision to see what we can do and how we can do it in the here and now as we move toward our hope. Wisdom does not confuse us; it brings lucidity to situations. We must take ownership of how we treat wisdom in our own lives, remaining humble and teachable. If we spend too much energy trying to manage others while never applying that opportunity for growth to ourselves, we will miss out on the treasure of refinement.

When applying wisdom, first and foremost apply it to yourself. As Jesus warned, don't get distracted by the splinter in someone else's eye when there might be a log in your own.

Eager in Hope

In this hope we were saved, but hope that is seen is not hope, because who hopes for what he sees? Now if we hope for what we do not see, we eagerly wait for it with patience.

ROMANS 8:24-25 CSB

Hope motivates us in action, but it also requires patience. Hope is future oriented. It isn't something that we can see or experience quite yet, and still, it moves us with desire in the here and now. It can be incredibly disheartening when we experience setbacks or are overwhelmed by the lack of control we have when it comes to timing. The vulnerability lies in the wait.

We can be eager in hope and still practice patience. We can do all that we know to do and still not move the needle on timing. Patience helps us to stay rooted in hope while not having to control the outcome. We can trust the Lord and his timing. Our eagerness reflects our desire, and our patience reflects our trust.

When you have done all that you know to do, trust the Lord. Put it in his hands. You can put your energy toward other things as you wait, for he is faithful and will not forget you.

Live in Hope

Just as you accepted Christ Jesus as your Lord, you must continue to follow him. Let your roots grow down into him, and let your lives be built on him. Then your faith will grow strong in the truth you were taught, and you will overflow with thankfulness.

COLOSSIANS 2:6-7 NLT

Ask any person who cultivates food, from a local gardener to a farmer, and they will tell you that fruitfulness requires hard work and patience. It requires attention and consistent care. If we want our lives to produce good fruit, we must approach our hearts like land that must be tended to.

One of the greatest ways to nourish hope in our lives is to be part of a community that supports it. Not every group will foster this, but finding one that does can be life changing. When we go through challenging times, the support of people and systems can give us greater strength and tools to endure them. Let's not neglect the importance of hopeful communities and spaces in our own lives or in what we offer others.

Connect with your support system today. If you don't have one, look into churches, support groups, or other places that may offer practical hope.

Promise to Return

> "I will not leave you as orphans;
> I am coming to you."
>
> JOHN 14:18 NASB

The choices we make may directly reflect what we value *and* our expectations of the future. If we don't have hope to guide us, we can lose sight of the meaning of what we're doing. Jesus promised that he wouldn't leave his disciples alone. They didn't yet know the profound statement he was making. Though he prepared them for his death, they still didn't seem to be ready when it happened. Hope was tested in the absence, not in his nearness.

However, Jesus did rise again and meet with his followers. He spent time with them, and he promised that the Holy Spirit would soon come and would never leave them. We are partakers in that promise today. The Spirit makes his home in us (1 Corinthians 3:16). As we live with the fellowship of the Holy Spirit as our comforter, teacher, and friend, we are reminded that Jesus will come again. This is not the end, and the fullness of his kingdom still awaits us, even as we wait for him.

The nearness of God is not a myth; it is a reality that you can taste, see, and know today. Invite the Spirit to nurture your hope and feed your soul.

Take What You Need

"I am with you and will watch over you wherever you go, and I will bring you back to this land. I will not leave you until I have done what I have promised you."

GENESIS 28:15 NIV

Depending on the day we're having or the season we are in, we may need more assurance in one area over another. When God told Jacob that he would be with him, perhaps he could have just stopped at that statement, but he didn't. He told Jacob that not only would he watch over him wherever he went, but he would also bring him back to that land. He promised to not leave him until his promises were completely satisfied.

God in his gracious love offers us more assurance than we expect. He promises to be with us, to go with us, and to return us to the places that he has prepared for us. He won't let up his presence from our lives until every promise he has made is fulfilled (hint: longer than our lifetime!). Whatever you need courage for today, find it in the persistent presence and help of your God and your savior. He is near!

Bring your anxieties to the Lord and receive strength and courage in the loving presence he pours over and into you.

Promised Fullness

You are complete in Him,
who is the head of all principality and power.

COLOSSIANS 2:10 NKJV

Every lack we have is met and overwhelmed in the fullness of Christ. We are made whole in him, wholly loved to life in his mercy. Colossians 2:9 says that the fullness of the deity (of God himself) is in Christ. Jesus Christ, the Son of God, and Son of Man, exudes the very nature of God.

We come to Christ as we are, and he meets us with abundance. We come in our weakness, and he welcomes us with his fullness. There isn't a need he can't meet, a wound he cannot heal, or a question he can't answer. We get to take him up on his invitation to rest in his presence. He offers us the help we need, and he directs us in his wisdom. His ways are not burdensome; they are light, for it is a shared yoke and a journey that he guides us into himself. What hope there is in his fellowship: fullness for our want, and strength for our weakness.

Instead of powering through your discomfort, bring it to the Lord. Ask him to meet you in your weakness with the overwhelming grace of his presence.

A Resting Place

Your life will be as bright as the noonday sun, and darkness will seem like morning. You will feel safe because there is hope; you will look around and rest in safety. You will lie down, and no one will scare you. Many people will want favors from you.

JOB 11:17-19 NCV

When we yield our hearts to the Lord, putting our hope in his faithful love, we find a resting place in him. There is no reason to fear, even when our lives turn upside down. Our safety and security are in the Lord and his faithfulness. We can rest assured that he will not leave us or forsake us, even in the painful periods of life. In fact, this promise was spoken to Job after he lost everything. He was grieving; this is when he needed hope the most.

When things are terrible, hope assures us that there is better ahead. The possibilities outweigh the awful reality. God's promises help us to look to the future with hope, and we can also cultivate hope in our own way. We can look for the meaning in our lives now and pick a goal outside of our reality to work toward. Let's not diminish the power hope can have to our resiliency and courage!

Encourage someone you know who is going through a tough time. Offer them respite, even for a moment, through an act of thoughtfulness, kindness, or service.

Ask Again

Lord, in my place of weakness and need,
I ask again: Will you come and help me?
I know I'm always in your thoughts.
You are my true Savior and hero,
so don't delay to deliver me now,
for you are my God.

PSALM 40:17 TPT

Healthy parents expect their children to come to them with their needs, as well as their requests. Good parents receive repeated requests with grace. God is the perfect parent; he is always patient, loving, and generous with us. We don't ever have to censor ourselves with him. No matter our experience with our earthly parents, God is always available and ready to help us when we turn to him.

King David did not hesitate to come to the Lord with all of his needs. He was called a friend of God. As God's children, and as his friends, we can rely on him in every season of the soul. Let's not let even our own mistakes keep us from his presence, for he is willing to save us as we yield to him. Hope may be in the reception you find in him today.

Humans need reminders. If there is someone in your life that you are waiting on to follow through, reach out to them with a gentle ask. If they don't come through this time, find a different route, but first ask again.

Until the Very End

"Behold, I am with you always,
to the end of the age."

MATTHEW 28:20 ESV

Hold out hope until the very end, not because it is wishful thinking, but because it is the motivation to keep on moving in purpose. Christ is with us; he is our strength. He is our promise, and his kingdom is our promised end. The presence of God with us is the power of God with us.

Hope does not put us to shame; it does not disappoint. There is every reason to hope because the Spirit dwells with us, and not only in theory but in practice. The Spirit is with us, the very power of God is with us, until the end of the age.

Put your life into perspective by remembering whose you are and what you are truly living for. Align your choices with that purpose as you receive from the unending strength of God's presence in you.

Lavish Love

Love consists in this: not that we loved God, but that he loved us and sent his Son to be the atoning sacrifice for our sins. Dear friends, if God loved us in this way, we also must love one another.

1 JOHN 4:10-11 CSB

God's love is the standard we should set all our love to. It is extravagant and kind. It is persistent and humble. It is powerful beyond measure. We are to love because we are so very loved. Like a cup overflowing, we give out of what we are filled with. We don't have to depend on our own strength, but on God's. Whatever is required of us is first offered us through Christ.

The love of God is like a well that we can visit at any time. We don't have to rely on yesterday's portion, for there is always fresh water to satisfy our souls and provide us with more than enough to offer others. The will and determination of hope is fueled by love, so let's drink deeply from the spring of God's presence today!

Choosing to love others becomes easier when you know how lavishly you are loved. Go straight to the source and fill up on the love of God; he delights in you, he offers you wisdom and grace, and he knows everything you need. Live from the overflow of his kindness today.

Ask Seek Knock

"Keep on asking, and you will receive what you ask for. Keep on seeking, and you will find. Keep on knocking, and the door will be opened to you. For everyone who asks, receives. Everyone who seeks, finds. And to everyone who knocks, the door will be opened."

MATTHEW 7:7-8 NLT

Persistence is a powerful trait. It keeps you moving toward what you have your heart set on. Studies show that students with high levels of hope put more effort into their goals and are persistent in working toward them. Unsurprisingly, this leads to higher grades. If we want to achieve our goals, having hope is paramount because it not only gives us something to reach for, but it also gives us the persistence to keep reaching for it even through obstacles.

Jesus invites us to keep on asking, keep on seeking, and keep on knocking. To those who do, he says, they will receive what they ask for, find what they look for, and walk through opened doors. If we easily give up, we miss out greatly. Life is not a series of easy steps, but when we know what we want and work toward it, we have the strength to endure until we meet our desired end.

Take this as your sign to keep on pushing toward the goals you have set. Don't give up but keep moving in that direction.

No Hesitation

"It will also come to pass that before they call, I will answer;
while they are still speaking, I will listen."

ISAIAH 65:24 NASB

God is ready and listening. Before the thought finishes, before
the words are even on your tongue, he knows your prayer.
Don't hesitate to come to him with every care today, for he
cares for you. He has time for you. He will not turn you away
or ask you to reach out at another time. He has both the
capacity and the desire to hear you now.

The higher our hope, the greater our quality of life; this is what
studies are showing. To have better levels of satisfaction, our
lives don't have to be perfect or pain free. We can struggle
with all sorts of challenges and still have a boost in how we
experience our lives as we harness hope. No matter where we
are today, it is the place of encounter. This is where God meets
us, where he answers our cries. He is ready with faithfulness,
wisdom, and grace to empower us to live abundantly.

As you reach out to God, also be the type of person who is
present when others bring you their cares. Take time to really
listen to the people in your life, putting the phone down and
the distractions away.

Effective and Powerful

Confess your sins to each other and pray for each other so that you may be healed. The prayer of a righteous person is powerful and effective.

JAMES 5:16 NIV

When we confess our struggles to others, there is a power in our unburdening. As we are met in that space, we can feel seen in our weakness. Instead of trying to power through in our own strength, which leads to feeling isolated, we can embrace the connective power of vulnerability. As we share ourselves with those we trust, we can also build trust by encouraging and praying for one another.

Those with support systems are shown to have higher levels of hope. We don't need a multitude of people that we trust with our most vulnerable selves; we just need a few. Being seen in our weakness is as important as being seen in our strength. There is powerful hope to be nurtured from a place of confession, encouragement, and support.

Identify who in your life you can be your most vulnerable self with. These are people who do not judge but meet you in your weakness and encourage you with practical and emotional support. Reach out in thanks to them today.

Living Under Grace

Sin shall not have dominion over you,
for you are not under law but under grace.

ROMANS 6:14 NKJV

The grace of God meets us in every moment. It empowers us to live with love, to choose the ways of God, and to receive the strength we need in our weakness. Grace fills the cracks that we cannot in our own efforts. It is the power of God at work in our lives. Grace is far more powerful than any habit of sin or mistake that we could ever make. It allows us to live in the freedom of God's favor. For these reasons, and so many more, grace is a wonderful gift.

Hope partners well with grace. Without hope, we may avoid bigger challenges, quit earlier on, and act helpless in the face of obstacles. Hope offers us a pathway to problem solving. With grace that covers our weaknesses, we are freed up to put our energy toward the hope that calls us forth. Living under grace allows us to shift our focus out of shame and allows us to see the things that entangle us from a different perspective while also giving us creative vision for solutions.

Is there something in your life that you feel has a strong hold over you that you wish it didn't? Ask for God's grace to cover that and give you vision to see the hope that creates a pathway to where you want to go.

Never Give Up

Jesus used this story to teach his followers that they should always pray and never lose hope.

LUKE 18:1 NCV

In verse 7 of the same chapter of Luke, Jesus said, "God will always give what is right to his people who cry to him night and day, and he will not be slow to answer them." We should always pray and never lose hope because God is righteous, he is quick to answer, and he is powerful to save.

Hope helps us to keep going, even when we face all sorts of challenges. It gives us the strength and motivation to endure because our focus remains on the possibility ahead, and the odds against us do not negate the power of our hope. If we want to grow in hope, practical exercises can help us do just that. Try one today.

Vividly imagine a goal that you have. Write down the possible obstacles you might face (the things that may stop you from achieving your goal). Make a few contingency plans to overcome those obstacles. Put it into action.

Weightier Matters

When you're joined to the Anointed One, circumcision and religious obligations can benefit you nothing. All that matters now is living in the faith that works and expresses itself through love.

GALATIANS 5:6 TPT

There is nothing wrong with tradition. It is when we find our identity, our hope, or our worth in that tradition that can trip us up. No tradition is equal to the power of God's love. Our salvation is not dependent upon us following a list of rules. It is entirely found within the grip of God's grace, which is a gift offered to all in the same measure.

Instead of being so caught up in the way things have been done, what if we looked with creativity at how we could live authentically in the love of God? If tradition and religious obligations were the way to know God, Jesus would have said as much. But that is not the message he proclaimed, and it certainly wasn't the one he died for. We cannot love our tradition more than we love people. We must make room for the messiness of love, grace, and faith, and allow them to take precedence over our preferred expression of godliness.

Jesus said that God looks at the heart. Allow room for creative expression of love and give up the need to hold others to a standard that God never put on them in the first place.

Spark of Faith

Faith comes from hearing,
and hearing through the word of Christ.

ROMANS 10:17 ESV

Faith does not appear out of thin air. It is sparked by something that we catch wind of. If we do not have the imagination that something is possible, how could we dream that it could be so?

Hope and faith go hand in hand. Faith is belief in what we cannot see, but is nonetheless real, and hope creates goals based on that faith. Hope harnesses the belief and creates pathways of possibility toward that end. Before we can have hope, we must have the spark of faith, and that spark comes through hearing. Listening to the testimonies of others can light a match that we tend to ourselves. Inspiration is not enough. It lights the spark, but hope harnesses the flame into a fire.

Inspirational listening can help build hope. Find an interview, podcast, or sermon that speaks to something you want to grow in hope in.

Plenty of Room

"Don't let your heart be troubled. Believe in God; believe also in me. In my Father's house are many rooms. If it were not so, would I have told you that I am going to prepare a place for you?"

JOHN 14:1-2 CSB

Jesus revealed the way to the Father. He did not come to shut the gate, but to open it to all who would enter. There is endless possibility in his kingdom. There is more reason to hope than we now know. There is grace to grow in faith, room to transform in love, and space for all who come to him.

When we feel closed in by our circumstances, it is all the more reason to look to Christ for hope. No challenge is impossible to overcome. In Christ, we find the fullness of God expressed in the humanity of Jesus. There is hope, always hope, for newness in him because of his resurrection life.

If you feel stuck in any area of your life, there is hope for breakthrough. Ask God to reveal the steps you can take to move out of action. If it is waiting that is required, don't be afraid to keep persevering in faith. There is so much room in God's kingdom, and he offers you open spaces in this life, as well.

Final Word

He will swallow up death forever! The Sovereign Lord will wipe away all tears. He will remove forever all insults and mockery against his land and people. The Lord has spoken!

ISAIAH 25:8 NLT

The Lord will have the final word over sin and death. He will wipe every tear from our eyes and forever remove the insults hurled against us. Even when we walk through the valley of the shadow of death, we don't need to fear evil for our God is with us. He will set every wrong right and his mercy and justice will have the final say.

It can be incredibly discouraging when injustices are not righted in the world and its systems. This does not mean that God is unjust, however. Romans 9:14 reminds us that God is not unfair. He shows mercy on whom he shows mercy and compassion on those he chooses. His love is unbiased and true. We can count on it, even until the very end.

As an act of faith, act justly, love mercy, and walk humbly with God (Micah 6:8). Whatever is in your power to do today, choose to be on the side of God's justice, which is often different than the world's.

Safe and Secure

In peace I will both lie down and sleep,
For You alone, Lord, have me dwell in safety.

PSALM 4:8 NASB

Hope allows us to endure hardship, but it also gives us reason to rest. Hope keeps us actively engaged in our lives, as it gives us something to work toward. At the end of the day, we need to rest. Good sleep can improve our mood, overall health, and brain performance. Healthy sleep hygiene leads to better days, and more energy to give to moving forward in hope.

When our nervous systems are overactive with anxiety, sleep becomes a challenge. Though we cannot guarantee good sleep in every season of our lives, we can do our best to set ourselves up well when it is in our power to do so. The feeling of safety is important to good sleep. When we create safe spaces that are quiet, dark, and optimal for sleep, we can more readily enter it. Laying our cares before the Lord is an important act of unburdening, as well, when we can receive the peace that God offers. Safe and secure, we can rest in peace.

Prioritize getting a good night's sleep every day this week. Limit screen time before bed, create a wind-down routine, and pray as you shut your eyes to sleep.

Faithful Guide

This God is our God for ever and ever;
he will be our guide even to the end.

PSALM 48:14 NIV

Through all time and space, beyond death, into eternity, this is how faithfully God will guide us. We don't have to fear death. Even when we meet our end on this earth, God guides us still.

Our hope, then, does not end when our bodies give out. Even when we breathe our last breath on this earth, we continue to follow the Lord into his kingdom. He will not let go of us. Let's hold on to him through every up and down of this life and continue to trust him with what comes next. There is none more faithful in love or more generous in kindness. He has so much more in store for us than we can imagine, and it is gloriously good!

What feelings come up when you think of the brevity of this life? Give God your fears and ask him for a glimpse of the goodness in store in the fullness of his kingdom.

Gracious Answers

The people shall dwell in Zion at Jerusalem;
You shall weep no more.
He will be very gracious to you at the sound of your cry;
When He hears it, He will answer you.

ISAIAH 30:19 NKJV

The passage today's verse comes from continues with the encouragement that even though we may be allowed to go through seasons of hardship and difficulty, God will be with us through it, and he won't hide himself from us. We can trust that God will continue to guide us, even when it is harder to see him.

Hope is as present in hard times as it is in the ease of good times. In fact, hope is even more necessary when we experience difficulties! God guides us with his voice as we turn to the right and to the left, giving us clues to the way to walk. We can trust his guidance and his wisdom to motivate us in hope. He really is reliable and graciously good in every season of the soul.

When hardships come, don't run away. Get still, ask the Lord for his wisdom and help, and move in the direction that seems right. Discernment will come as you move!

Integrity Matters

The wicked are ruined by their own evil,
but those who do right are protected even in death.

PROVERBS 14:32 NCV

When we do the right thing, we are protected in that choice. Even when we are persecuted for it, God honors the commitment to follow his ways. Romans 1:17 reminds us, "those who are right with God will live by faith."

If we are to live by faith in Christ, we will also choose to follow the path of his love in every area of our lives. Integrity keeps us honest, honorable, and fair. Though we are far from perfect, we remain humble in love; willing to admit when we've got it wrong and make our best effort to do better. Thank God that righteousness is from him; we have only to believe. And if we believe, we will live it out.

Do the right thing, even when no one else is looking. Do the loving thing even when it is inconvenient.

Shadow of Kindness

Let your love and steadfast kindness
overshadow us continually,
for we trust and we wait upon you!

PSALM 33:22 TPT

As we wait upon the Lord, trusting him to faithfully follow through on his Word, we are under the shadow of his kindness and the covering of his love. Our hope may be put to test in the waiting, but that is where the power is. We are empowered by grace to press on and to create new plans to keep going. Even as we wait, we are completely immersed in the kindness of God's presence to imagine new breakthroughs for our problems.

What would it look like for us to extend kindness to others in their own waiting periods? Can we become spaces of safety and hope for those who need it? As we partner with God's heart, we can offer love, understanding, and support to those in need of a fresh dose of hope. As we trust and wait upon God, we learn to offer the lovingkindness we experience to others.

Intentionally dwell in the kindness of God and extend that to others wherever they are at today. Remember that it is under love that you bloom, and that love is your source and easily shared.

In Every Way

May the Lord of peace himself give you peace at all times
in every way. The Lord be with you all.

2 THESSALONIANS 3:16 ESV

The presence of God is tangible and real. It is full of palpable
peace. No matter what we are going through, the peace of
God can meet us. It can cover, fill, and overflow us. Peace
causes our hearts to calm, our nervous systems to regulate,
and our bodies to rest. It gives our minds clarity. We don't
have to rush to judgment because we have the space to make
wise decisions.

In every circumstance and in every possible way, the
presence of God can pervade us with his peace. There isn't a
circumstance too complicated or a situation too overwhelming
that God's peace cannot meet us there. What hope we have
with God's presence ever so near!

*Every time you need a fresh dose of peace today, close your
eyes, take a deep breath, and turn your attention to the Spirit
of God. Invite his peace in with your breath.*

Ultimate Transformation

Our citizenship is in heaven, and we eagerly wait for a Savior from there, the Lord Jesus Christ. He will transform the body of our humble condition into the likeness of his glorious body, by the power that enables him to subject everything to himself.

PHILIPPIANS 3:20-21 CSB

It may be out of our ability to experience some hopes that we have in this life, but that does not mean those hopes are invalid. We all want to be healthy, though we will struggle with the limitations of our bodies at some point. We want success, but there are barriers that we cannot push through on our own. Even when our ideas of a good life fall short, there is a promised transformation that will not disappoint.

In the fullness of God's eternal kingdom, we will know satisfaction like we cannot imagine. The glimpses of goodness we experience in this life are no less meaningful in light of that. They are each a gift, and a glimpse, from the generous heart of a good father. Let's remember our identity as God's children and live with the confidence of his kindness by showing it to others.

You cannot control how many days you have, nor can you manipulate the challenges you face. However, you can choose how you live and respond. Choose kindness, generosity, peace, and joy in all things today.

Convinced of Goodness

I am confident I will see the LORD's goodness
while I am here in the land of the living.
Wait patiently for the LORD. Be brave and courageous.
Yes, wait patiently for the LORD.

PSALM 27:13-14 NLT

When we live with the conviction that God's goodness will meet us in the land of the living, we will have eyes to see it. Especially in hard times, reminding ourselves of the imminent goodness of God's powerful presence can be an incredible boost to our hope. It can give us the resilience we need to keep trusting and waiting for the breakthrough we so long for.

Courage isn't required when there is no challenge to face. Courage is necessary as we face the unknown. When we step out into uncharted territory, we don't know what will meet us. But of this we can be sure: God's goodness is there, just as surely as it is with us now!

Today's verse is an incredible encouragement, especially in grief, transition, and in the face of any unknown. Memorize it and come back to it throughout your day.

My Redeemer Lives

"I know that my Redeemer lives, And at the last,
He will take His stand on the earth."

JOB 19:25 NASB

Job would not let his faith be diminished by his circumstances. He wouldn't let his confidence in God be overwhelmed by his grief. Even when all in his life felt like a complete failure, Job still proclaimed in faith that his Redeemer lives. Can we do the same in our disappointment and troubles?

When we set our eyes of faith on the everlasting power of God, we shift our perspective from the temporal to the eternal. Though we struggle now, God remains merciful. Though we experience great loss, our Redeemer lives. He will take his stand on the earth. We will stand before him and see him with our own eyes. Let our hearts take hold of that hope, even as we remind our souls of God's power.

Take every opportunity—every struggle, frustration, and question—to proclaim "I know that my Redeemer lives" over your own heart. As you remind yourself of his presence and power, harness the hope that arises.

Sweet Pursuit

You have been my hope, Sovereign LORD,
my confidence since my youth.
As for me, I will always have hope;
I will praise you more and more.

PSALM 71:5,14 NIV

God's powerful presence is available to us in every moment. No matter how long we have followed him, his faithfulness remains, and his truth does, too. Looking over our journey of faith can be the encouragement we need to keep pursuing God. Where has God come through for us? What has he done to instill confidence in our hearts as we follow him?

We pursue the things that are valuable to us. Hope is a fierce motivator, for it marries belief with desire. It can be an incredible intervention for our emotional wellbeing. Let's not overlook the power of looking to the past to garner courage for our future. Those who have tasted and seen the kindness of God will be motivated to experience even more of it as they pursue him with their hearts filled with hope.

If you have journals or notes from your earlier walk with the Lord, revisit them. If you don't, simply walk down memory lane and ask the Spirit to highlight how God met you, provided for you, and sowed his goodness into your life.

November

I am certain that God, who
began the good work within you,
will continue his work until
it is finally finished on the day
when Christ Jesus returns.

PHILIPPIANS 1:6 NLT

Evidence for Hope

The Lord knows how to deliver the godly out of temptations and to reserve the unjust under punishment for the day of judgment.

2 PETER 2:9 NKJV

God rescued Lot from the destruction of Sodom, and he knows how to rescue us from our trials and temptations, too. We don't have to be perfect to experience the power of God's salvation. In fact, the very need we have for him is evidence that God's grace is necessary. We depend on him, and he is faithful to help us.

The evidence for hope is in the breakthroughs of all those who experience it. It is walked out, tested, and tried, and found to be helpful. Hope is living and active, and it changes us as we move in it. Constructive hope allows us to make progress. But that's not all; constructive hope paired with constructive doubt, which simply means the reality we are facing, can lead to the spark that makes us active participants in creating change. The evidence for hope lies in the movement toward it.

Partner with God's power by harnessing hope through seeing where the intersection of progress being made, and the reality of the hardship lies. There is always a path forward; no problem is without possibility for breakthrough.

Discerning the Season

There is a time for everything,
and everything on earth has its special season.

ECCLESIASTES 3:1 NCV

There is wisdom in knowing the season you are in. Ecclesiastes says that there is a time for everything on earth. We cannot do everything at the same time; this is wise to recognize so that we have our perspectives where they need to be. If we spend our energy weeding when we should be planting, for instance, we work against the timing of the season we are in.

It is much better to know what our energies are best put toward right now. We can plan, but we cannot overlook the importance of engaging in the work that is needed now. Hope connects the two. We can plan for what lies ahead while taking the steps to get there. It keeps things in proper perspective.

When was the last time you reconsidered where you were pouring your energy? Look at the lay of the land of your life now. What is required to get to where you want to be? What can you do now to nurture that?

Reliable Foundation

Jesus, the Anointed One, is always the same—yesterday, today, and forever. So don't let anyone lead you astray with all sorts of novel and exotic teachings. It is more beautiful to feast on grace and be inwardly strengthened than to be obsessed with dietary rules which in themselves have no lasting benefit.

HEBREWS 13:8-9 TPT

Jesus Christ is the same yesterday, today, and forever. He is the firm foundation of our faith, and his teachings are as applicable to our lives today as they were when he first spoke to them. He spoke in stories so that the people who listened to him would understand. The truth of his law of love remains, and it is not too difficult to apply to our lives.

Instead of getting so caught up in the form and function of our faith, when we choose to build our faith upon Christ and following him on his path of mercy, we can live in the freedom his grace offers. His ways are not easy, but they are simple. And his grace is always available to help us.

When you look at your hopes, the little and big ones, what do they point toward when it comes to your foundation? What values do they reflect? Go to God with every dream and hope you have and be sure to build your life on the foundation of his nature and values, emulating them in your own life.

Remember Who He Is

Bless the Lord, O my soul, and forget not all his benefits,
who forgives all your iniquity, who heals all your diseases,
who redeems your life from the pit,
who crowns you with steadfast love and mercy,
who satisfies you with good so that your youth
is renewed like the eagle's.

PSALM 103:2-5 ESV

What miracles of kindness God sows in the lives of those who look to him. He is faithful in love. He forgives, heals, redeems, and satisfies us. He is better than we could dare to dream—no, really! When we look back through eyes of faith, can we not recognize where his mercy sowed miracles into our story?

When we choose to bless the Lord, not forgetting what he has done, but celebrating each miracle, we join our hearts with his faithfulness. We can praise him for his goodness and faithfulness. We can rejoice in the wonders his love has revealed in our lives. What a glorious God he is, so loyal in love and outstanding in power!

Hope creatively looks to the future for possibilities you have not yet known. Your past victories can strengthen your ability to hope. Write down every blessing you can think of in your life, every breakthrough you've experienced, and thank God for each one!

Thoroughly Equipped

All Scripture is inspired by God and is profitable for teaching, for rebuking, for correcting, for training in righteousness, so that the man of God may be complete, equipped for every good work.

2 TIMOTHY 3:16-17 CSB

If we want to be equipped for every good work in this life, we cannot ignore the wisdom and instruction that the Scriptures offer us. There is so much benefit in allowing the Word of God to challenge, correct, and direct us. We must be sure to remember that Jesus is the Living Word, too, and his teachings direct us to the very nature of God.

As we act and follow through on what we say we will do, we are both satisfied in our effort and motivated to continue. The Word of God helps us to stay clear on how we should live, move, and act. Humility is necessary so that we remain open and teachable, learning as we go. We go from glory to glory, as 2 Corinthians 3:18 puts it, as we continually transform into the image of God with us through the alignment of our lives with his.

Inspiration is a necessary aspect of hope, and so is endurance. Find inspiration in the Word of God today and follow through on its leading.

All Things New

The one sitting on the throne said, "Look, I am making everything new!" And then he said to me, "Write this down, for what I tell you is trustworthy and true."

REVELATION 21:5 NLT

Hope is predicated on the possibility of experiencing something new. Hope reaches into the future, into what we have not yet known, and it motivates us to act in the present to move toward it. If we believe that all things are possible for those who believe, then we will not hesitate to believe for what God promised.

God's promises are trustworthy and true. All that he has said, he will do. He really is that faithful, that trustworthy, and that good. Let's not neglect the power of putting our hope in the one who is able to make everything new. When we align our thoughts with his kingdom, we will not stay stuck or in despair of the circumstances we now live in. Though we do not deny reality, we recognize that God is able to create new possibilities. He is not finished working miracles in his mercy; he is still making things new, and he will continue to do it!

Where there is a challenge, there is possibility for breakthrough. Align your hope with the faithfulness of God and his incomparable power. Allow his truth to direct your faith.

Wisdom and Power

"May the name of God be blessed forever and ever, For wisdom and power belong to Him. It is He who changes the times and the periods; He removes kings and appoints kings; He gives wisdom to wise men, And knowledge to people of understanding."

DANIEL 2:20-21 NASB

Wisdom and power belong to God. He is the father of creation, setting everything in its place. The universe is still expanding today; it is this God who set that into motion! Revelation 5:13 describes every creature, everywhere, joining and saying, "To Him who sits on the throne and to the Lamb be the blessing, the honor, the glory, and the dominion forever and ever."

If we truly believe that God is all-powerful and full of lovingkindness, then we will not hesitate to ask him for what we need, and even what we long for. He has an endless portion to offer us, so let's not keep our eyes down looking for scraps when he invites us to sit at the table of his abundant feast!

Pray big prayers, asking God to give you boldness and vision for more as he reveals his incomparable nature to you.

Higher Understanding

God made the earth by his power;
he founded the world by his wisdom
and stretched out the heavens by his understanding.

JEREMIAH 10:12 NIV

There is so much wisdom in God. As we give our lives to him, he offers us practical help and faith to believe for more than we've yet experienced. He expands our understanding as we submit our hearts to him. Often, the greatest awakenings we experience are through hardship and suffering, so we should not be surprised when our faith is tested in these waters. God promises to be with us, and he offers us his own higher perspective to help us through.

Perseverance is motivated by hope because we look past our troubles to the joy that awaits us on the other side. This is a better way of looking at things. Studies show that people with high levels of hope see challenges as an opportunity for growth. Every stretching of our beliefs, hearts, and perspectives, is an opportunity to grow in grace, mercy, and faith.

Consider if there is any area of your life that would benefit from a perspective shift. Hope often motivates perseverance, so don't be afraid to set your goals beyond what you now have.

Hone Your Skills

Do you see a man who excels in his work?
He will stand before kings;
He will not stand before unknown men.

PROVERBS 22:29 NKJV

There is incredible value in honing our skills through hard work. Raw talent can get us so far, but dedication paired with skill will take us far in life. Consistent effort brings us reward. We cannot wish ourselves into favorable places, though we can certainly trust that God will take our effort and honor it.

Hope is not a wish. It is a goal that motivates us in action. It is good to work hard and dedicate ourselves to excelling in our skills. This does not mean we find our worth in what we do, but we can find great satisfaction in it. Hope, too, can help us find new paths that others have not treaded. It is necessary for innovation because hope sees possibility and accounts for challenges that may arise; it is a problem-solving pathway.

Make sure that you are not just coasting on your skill; put the work in to get even better at it. Your effort will not go unrewarded.

Revelations in Nature

There are things about him that people cannot see—his eternal power and all the things that make him God. But since the beginning of the world those things have been easy to understand by what God has made. So people have no excuse for the bad things they do.

ROMANS 1:20 NCV

If we need a fresh revelation of who God is, take this as an invitation to go out in nature. Is there a place that feels sacred to you, or a natural feature that makes you feel your small place in the world? Nature can help us put ourselves into perspective. Standing by a large body of water, gazing at a star-filled sky, or walking among ancient trees can all help us to remember that there was so much before us, and even more will continue after we are gone. Even more, God is the one who created this world and everything in it.

It can be a relief to remember that the universe does not revolve around our lives, not our successes or our losses. It goes on around us. Witnessing the changes of the seasons can remind us that nothing lasts forever, and neither will our suffering. This is a concrete way to connect to hope.

Take time to be outside today, even if just for a few undistracted minutes. Pay attention to nature, and let it be your teacher.

Living Poetry

We have become his poetry, a re-created people that will
fulfill the destiny he has given each of us, for we are joined
to Jesus, the Anointed One. Even before we were born,
God planned in advance our destiny and the good works
we would do to fulfill it!

EPHESIANS 2:10 TPT

When we are young, we imagine the trajectory of our lives as
a straight line. However, life does not work this way. There will
be unforeseen challenges that arise and set us in a different
direction than we imagined. This does not mean that we are
off course, simply that the course looks more circuitous than
we originally thought.

Our lives are like living poetry being written as we experience
it. We get to choose how we engage in every moment,
submitting our hearts in humility to the one who created them.
We can trust his loving hand and his wise guidance. Instead of
being discouraged by living a different reality than we thought
we would, can we find the beauty within it?

*Take time to really think about the parts of your life that are
surprisingly beautiful. Give thanks, open your heart in hope,
and embrace the life that is now yours.*

Inspired Thoughts

Behold, he who forms the mountains and creates the wind, and declares to man what is his thought, who makes the morning darkness, and treads on the heights of the earth— the LORD, the God of hosts, is his name!

AMOS 4:13 ESV

The God who created the universe, who still forms mountains, sets winds in motion, and thoughtfully displays each sunrise and sunset is the God who shares his thoughts with us. He reveals his wisdom to us through the fellowship of his living Word. He offers us insight when we are stumped, help when we are in trouble, and beauty for our ashes. He is incredibly kind, patient, and powerful.

He is also accessible. Even if our need seems small, no request is insignificant. When we need a fresh dose of inspiration, God offers us the power of his perspective. What hope we find in him whenever we come before him!

Ask for God's thoughts when you find you need a different perspective. He is overflowing in wisdom, and just one word from him can inspire you in creative ways.

Dry Bones

"This is what the Lord GOD says to these bones: I will
cause breath to enter you, and you will live. I will put
tendons on you, make flesh grow on you, and cover you
with skin. I will put breath in you so that you come to life.
Then you will know that I am the LORD."

EZEKIEL 37:5-6 CSB

Nothing is impossible for God. He can take our dry bones and
breathe life into them, causing us to come to life. He turns
hearts of stone into hearts of flesh, melting our defenses and
healing our trauma. He can transform us from the inside out,
giving us the abundance of his lifegiving love to minister to
the deepest places of our soul.

The Lord offers new life for all who come to him. He is not
stingy with his grace; he is more generous than anyone who
has ever lived. With this in mind, we can come to him with
hearts wide open, trusting him to take care of us and revive us.
He really is that good, trustworthy, and powerful.

Speak lifegiving encouragement to those around you.

Deep Understanding

Have you never heard? Have you never understood?
The LORD is the everlasting God, the Creator of all the earth.
He never grows weak or weary.
No one can measure the depths of his understanding.

ISAIAH 40:28 NLT

God, in all of his matchless wisdom and incredible strength, is not only the everlasting God, but he is present with us. He is not a far-off God who lives in the sky. His Spirit dwells with us. It is almost too much to imagine: that our Creator is not only God, but God with us.

Knowing that God is with us, we have a permanent source of hope that helps us to look positively toward the future with the tools we need to persist through hard times. *No one can measure the depths of his understanding*. He freely gives us the solutions we need, offering us the wisdom of his kingdom to help us get unstuck and to keep moving in the liberty of his love. Let's go to him for all that we need, not neglecting to apply the practicality of his wisdom to our lifestyles and interactions.

You don't need all the answers to take the next right step. Sometimes wisdom and understanding unfold as you take inspired steps, with God revealing the power of his nature through them. Ask for God's understanding to apply to an area of your life and walk it out today.

Prime Example

"I gave you an example, so that you also would do just as I did for you."

JOHN 13:15 NASB

The life of Jesus is more than a story. It is more than a picture of God's powerful mercy. It is an example that we can and should follow. Right before Jesus told his disciples that he had given them an example to follow, he had washed their feet. In many cultures today, the significance of this act is lost. In Jesus' day, servants would wash the feet of guests, wiping away the grime of the outside. It was not an enviable task; it was one of the most humble.

Jesus wants us to follow his loving lead by being willing to serve each other with humble hearts. The hope of his kingdom is not in how much wealth we store for ourselves now; in fact, in many ways, this goes against his teachings. We are to be generous, humble, kind, and honest, the most trustworthy and loving people on this planet. It is worth it to follow his example. If we don't, can we truly call ourselves followers of Christ?

Go into your day with the commitment to see ways you can serve others in love. Don't let pride dictate your actions; let the example of Jesus guide you!

Safe Harbors

"Blessed are the meek, for they will inherit the earth."

MATTHEW 5:5 NIV

When we remain humble, not holding too tightly to the things of this earth, we leave room for a better and brighter hope. Relationships are more important than stuff. How we treat others is more important than what we collect. Our character development is of primary importance, not only to us, but to God, as well. Let's be sure to spend as much energy, if not more, on developing our character as we do on building a portfolio.

The term *meek* is used in many older translations of the Bible. It can mean humble, gentle, or mild. Gentleness is an important attribute of any approachable person. Mildness does not equal dullness; it can mean safe, in this instance. Humble, approachable, gentle people are safe harbors in this world.

Are you a safe person for people to come to? Are you able to listen to others with openness and direct them in gentleness? Consider who is a safe harbor for you to find rest in their company. Try to be that for people in your life, as well.

Don't Forget Delight

Go, eat your bread with joy,
And drink your wine with a merry heart;
For God has already accepted your works.

ECCLESIASTES 9:7 NKJV

God doesn't disapprove of you enjoying what you have in life. This is important to recognize, otherwise you may fall into the trap of thinking that you must be apologetic or guilty when you experience pleasure in the little things. Pleasure is a gift from God, so go ahead and delight in the life you have! Eat your food with joy and drink your refreshments with gladness.

If we put off delighting in the simple things, what is the purpose of hope? If we endlessly reach for what we don't have, we miss out on the satisfaction of what is already ours. As we learn to really embrace with joy what is ours here and now, we can look ahead with even more hope, confident hope, for goodness to meet us in the future.

Be intentional about enjoying the little pleasures of your day. God delights in you, and he loves to see you delight in the beauty of life. Don't be afraid to experience these pleasures, for they are a gift from God!

Lifetime of Kindness

His anger lasts only a moment,
but his kindness lasts for a lifetime.
Crying may last for a night,
but joy comes in the morning.

PSALM 30:5 NCV

What we know of God's character reflects in our thoughts about him and our expectations of him. If we feel that he is distant and disapproving, we will look for the confirmation of those traits in our lives. We may start to act the same way to others. But if we know God as kind, merciful, and near, we will see his goodness around us. We will be more apt to treat others with kindness and presence.

Though we cannot escape the grief of loss or the painful parts of life, we can know God's kindness in it. As we look ahead to the sunrise and fresh start of a new day, we can meet it with the hope of God's redemption meeting us in it.

Reflect on who you believe God to be and what you expect of him. Ask him to reveal himself in kindness and to transform your expectations of him in the faithfulness of his love toward you.

Mirror that Delight

Find your delight and true pleasure in Yahweh,
and he will give you what you desire the most.

PSALM 37:4 TPT

As you delight yourself in the Lord, you may find that the tenderness you feel toward him is simply a reflection of his loving care toward you. It is easier to reciprocate kindness toward those who are kind to us than to choose tender care toward those who treat us poorly. The beautiful thing about our relationship with the Lord is that he fills us up, and we get to mirror what he does for us right back to him.

In gratitude for what we receive, we partner with God in choosing to walk with him. Partnership and gratitude, this is what God expects of us. This is not too much to ask!

Give God the gratitude of a heart that recognizes his grace. Walk with him, following his ways; his yoke is easy, and his burden is light! Simplify the expectations you have of yourself, and simply partner with him. Also, taking time to listen to what God says over you, speak those words right back to him in a reciprocal prayer.

Joyful Strength

> "Go your way. Eat the fat and drink sweet wine and send portions to anyone who has nothing ready, for this day is holy to our Lord. And do not be grieved, for the joy of the LORD is your strength."

NEHEMIAH 8:10 ESV

We often complicate God's Word by adding distinctions that God never meant for us. Following him is simple, as is his wisdom, but it is not always the easy route. The more time we spend getting to know the Lord in his kindness, generosity, and faithfulness, the more natural it becomes to be more like him. As we go on our way, gaining nourishment from our portion and generously sharing with those who have none, we live out his grace. When we need courage and strength, we can find it in the joy of the Lord over us and through us!

When we know how wonderfully and wholly we are loved, what confidence is ours! The joy of the Lord is our strength because we know that he delights in us and that means we don't have to second guess our identity in him. Walking in the confidence of being loved is not arrogance; it is our birthright, our joy, and our freedom!

Ask the Holy Spirit to reveal what God thinks of you, who he says you are. Walk confidently in that identity and be generous in kindness to others today.

Nurture the Gift

Don't neglect the gift that is in you;
it was given to you through prophecy,
with the laying on of hands by the council of elders.

1 TIMOTHY 4:14 CSB

When we take active participation in nurturing the gifts, talents, skills, and resources that have been given to us we become faithful stewards, walking in wisdom, and moving in hope. Before we can even venture to manage others, we must manage ourselves first. Part of good self-management is using what we have to serve others.

As we nurture our giftings through time and attention, we can grow them even more as we put them into practice in service. A key aspect of having hope is tending to the goals we have by taking steps toward them. This, too, is nurture. It is active participation in reaching the ends we want to see. Partnership is a powerful gift, but our control and effort are our own to manage.

Make a plan of action when it comes to an area that you want to grow. Don't overlook the power of sowing into your strengths.

Enjoy the Fruit

I concluded there is nothing better than to be happy and enjoy ourselves as long as we can. And people should eat and drink and enjoy the fruits of their labor, for these are gifts from God.

ECCLESIASTES 3:12-13 NLT

If we endlessly work ourselves as if on a hamster wheel, we miss out on the satisfaction and celebration of tasting the fruits of our labor. If we constantly move from one completed task onto the next, we may find that delight remains elusive. Taking time to enjoy the fruit of our labor is a sweet joy. It is not something we should neglect!

We grow in hope as we experience the fulfillment of others. If we move on too quickly, we miss out on the glorious delight, celebration, and joy of what we worked for. Nothing tastes better than a freshly picked fruit or vegetable. How much more delight if what we eat is something we grew ourselves! As we delight in the fruit, we often find that there is plenty to share. What a gift it is to see the fruits of our labor and to be able to share it with others!

Take time to celebrate your wins—completed projects, hard things done, accomplishments made—no matter how small or how big. Whatever makes you take the time to enjoy and recognize it, do it!

Eternal Goodness

Give thanks to the LORD, for He is good,
For His mercy is everlasting.

PSALM 107:1 NASB

What we focus our attention on, we find. If we go into our day looking for reasons to be grateful, we will find them. If we set an intention to see beauty in the world around us, we will see it. We could learn from children, who go about the world at a slower pace. They know how to engage with awe and wonder in a way that we must work at. But there is good news; if we cultivate it, we can also experience the awe and wonder of the world through our imagination.

The goodness of God is not elusive. It is present wherever he is present. Kindness exudes from his nearness; mercy kisses our hearts with the power of God's presence. There are so many reasons to give thanks to the Lord. Find as many as you can today. Write them down, share them with others, or record them in a creative way. Only do the searching; if you do, you will find them!

Take an awe walk: one where you let your attention be drawn to anything that pulls at it. A flower in the sidewalk, a child interacting with an animal, the way the sun hits the clouds, that expansive space of wonder is available as you take the time to find it.

Hope of Breakthrough

Many, Lord, are asking, "Who will bring us prosperity?"
Let the light of your face shine on us.
Fill my heart with joy when their grain and new wine
abound.

Psalm 4:6-7 NIV

Though others may doubt our hope, it is not theirs to dictate. It is also not theirs to cultivate. As we continue to put our trust in the Lord, we can put our hope into action by walking in faith and choosing to partner with God's purposes. Hope is not elusive. It is necessary for an abundant life, for it helps us to persevere with resilience through the hard times and allows us to taste the satisfaction of goodness where it already meets us.

We have no reason to be ashamed of hope. It is an incredible motivator, and it is also unique to each of us. Though we may share a hope with others, there are others that remain our own. This is both normal and important. Instead of letting the doubt and differing priorities of others discourage us in our hopes, let's be sure to glean the courage and encouragement of the brave ones who pave their own paths in wild places. There is the promise of breakthrough as we keep going!

It is important to know the driving force behind your hope and to really take ownership of the hope you have. Join your hope to God's faithfulness and let go of the opinions of those who don't want the same things.

Such Wonderful Things

Only fear the LORD, and serve Him in truth with all your heart; for consider what great things He has done for you.

1 SAMUEL 12:24 NKJV

As we reflect on the miracles of his mercy that have met us in the details of our story, they become seeds of hope for the goodness of God to continue to meet us in our journey.

Our best days are not behind us. Though we may have tasted and seen the goodness of the Lord, there is far more to nourish our hearts in hope as we continue to follow him. We have only seen a glimpse of his glory; there is so much more to discover in the realm of his lavish love! Let's not give up hope for our lives, for there is so much grace, plentiful peace, and jubilant joy to still uncover in fellowship with the King of kings.

When you find yourself discouraged by how things are going, take some time to reflect on the great things God has already done for you. What beauty have you known in life? What overwhelming joy or relief? Take heart and take hope; there is much more where that came from.

Blessed to See

"You are blessed, because you see with your eyes and hear with your ears."

MATTHEW 13:16 NCV

At one point or another, we will come to a dead end where once we saw a pathway. When that happens, hope can help us imagine a different way. It is an incredible resource to get us unstuck through creative problem solving. It's not a question of whether challenges will present themselves on our path, but when. When we know this, we can anticipate the need to lean into hope to encourage us.

Hope is the ability to see into the future, into what is not yet a reality, and implement strategies to get us there. We are blessed when we have vision to see what others can't. We are blessed to hear wisdom when others hear only noise. When we set our hearts on God to guide us in hope, he opens our eyes to see the light of his presence. He gives us the wisdom we need to get through the obstacles of our faith. Certainly, we are blessed in hope.

Do you want to give up at the first sign of difficulty? Or do you welcome the challenges with an open heart, trusting God to guide you through them? Write down a goal you have and some potential obstacles that may arise. Come up with a game plan to deal with these obstacles.

Always Thankful

In the midst of everything be always giving thanks,
for this is God's perfect plan for you in Christ Jesus.

1 Thessalonians 5:18 tpt

Gratitude can help us grow in hope as it encourages our hearts in what is already good. It can raise our expectations of hope for the future as we engage with the beauty of answered prayers, simple pleasures, and encouraging presence. There are always reasons to give thanks. Today is no different.

Thankfulness keeps our hearts connected to the giver of good gifts. It directs our attention in meaningful ways to find glimmers of goodness, even during hardship. No season is without its gift. No circumstance is purely bad or purely good; it is often a mix of many factors and feelings. We can resist discouragement by turning our eyes to what is true, beautiful, spacious, and present right here and now in this moment. As we do, our ability to look ahead with hope will be strengthened.

Even rejection can be reason to give thanks if nothing more than it isn't for you. In whatever you experience today, give thanks. The more you practice it, the more natural it will become, and your heart will respond in hope.

Direct Your Attention

"Where your treasure is,
there your heart will be also."

MATTHEW 6:21 ESV

Our hearts follow the things we treasure. We pursue that which is valuable to us. This is as true of our hopes as anything else in life. If we want to succeed in attaining our goals, we need to be sure of the value of them.

Value can be cultivated, and it can also change throughout our lives. Though we may work hard to successfully get that degree, start that business, or achieve whatever goal we strive for, none of it matters if we lose ourselves in the process. We can have these goals, work toward them, and remain connected to our identity. If we put our treasure in following the law of God's love and in knowing him, we will not be disappointed in the end. We can build our character and work on building our skills, as well. It all goes together in his kingdom.

Spend time visualizing what is most important to you today and this week. After you get clear on your goals, make sure you are putting the energy toward them and saying no to other things when necessary.

Share What You Have

You will be enriched in every way for all generosity,
which produces thanksgiving to God through us.

2 CORINTHIANS 9:11 CSB

Generosity is a kingdom value. It is not an afterthought or
option. It is a core tenet of God's nature and of how he wants
us to live out his love on the earth. We are blessed to be a
blessing. We are enriched to generously share with others. We
cannot hoard our resources and still claim to be following the
law of God's love wholeheartedly.

Being intentional in generosity is a builder of hope in others.
As we share what we have, we spread out the resources so that
all may partake and give thanks. Far be it from us to withhold
what God so willingly offers. Where there is greed, there is
pride, and where pride is, there is an invitation to either humble
ourselves or be humbled. Communities that support and uplift
one another foster a culture of hope. We can choose how we
live, but we cannot avoid the mandate of God to be others-
minded and generous, especially if we have a lot!

Determine what area of your life you want to be more
generous in and share your practical resources in that area
this coming day, week, and month.

Wholehearted Trust

The LORD is my strength and shield.
I trust him with all my heart.
He helps me, and my heart is filled with joy.
I burst out in songs of thanksgiving.

PSALM 28:7 NLT

A strong sense of trust and community have been shown to foster hope in those recovering from substance abuse. We cannot ignore the importance of trust in the people around us to build deeper relationships and to encourage us in resilient hope. Even when we don't know who to trust, God is faithful and true, and he will come through for us. He gives us wisdom to connect to the right people.

What relief comes from the help we find when we need it. What joy bubbles up in a grateful heart! When we put our trust in the Lord, that hope will not be left unsatisfied. He always comes through for us. It is so important that we build a sense of trust in safe spaces and communities, as well. If we want to thrive in hope, belonging to groups that encourage us, accept us, and offer support when we need it are so very important.

Engage in a group, community, or with a person that is safe to share your struggles with, and not only your strengths.

December

The eyes of the L{\small ORD}
are on those who fear him,
on those whose hope
is in his unfailing love.

P{\small SALM} 33:18 {\small NIV}

Dependable Shepherd

Like a shepherd He will tend His flock,
In His arm He will gather the lambs
And carry them in the fold of His robe;
He will gently lead the nursing ewes.

ISAIAH 40:11 NASB

God is dependable to faithfully care for those who rely on him. He is a shepherd that fights off the enemy and goes after the lost lambs. He doesn't forget a single sheep in his care. You can be sure that he has not forgotten you. He knows every struggle and every obstacle in your path. He will gather you in his arms and carry you in his robe. He is always gentle toward his people.

Just because God is gentle does not mean that he is weak. It is important that we recognize the strength of love in our own lives, too. Kindness is not weakness, and we should not expect the leaders in our lives to rule with pride, force, or manipulation. You can be sure that if they do, they are not reflecting God's leadership. Let's be like him in kindness, intention, and care, and let's also be like him in confidence.

Don't back down from your hope in God. Let it root you in the identity of Christ and in his ways.

Power of Faith

Abram believed the LORD,
and he credited it to him as righteousness.

GENESIS 15:6 NIV

Did you realize the power of your faith? When we take God at his word and follow him with surrendered hearts, we trust him to follow through in his faithfulness, even when our hopes are far off. There are some hopes that we can partner with, and there are others that remain out of our control. All we can do is activate our faith and put our trust in God. In these times, God credits our faith as righteousness.

We have nothing to fear when we follow the Lord. He promises to fulfill every vow he has made, and he will. As we trust him with our lives, we put our hope in his unfailing nature.

Is there a hope that you cannot do anything more about today? Put your faith in God and trust him to follow through in faithfulness. He can do far more than you can ask or imagine!

Christ Our Banner

"In that day there shall be a Root of Jesse, Who shall stand as a banner to the people; For the Gentiles shall seek Him, And His resting place shall be glorious."

Isaiah 11:10 NKJV

The promise of Christ's redemption is not only for those born into the faith. It wasn't just for the Hebrew nation, either. It is for all people, everywhere. The invitation stands open for all to come to him, to stand under the banner of his mercy and receive forgiveness and strength. The plan was in place from the beginning, so we should not be surprised by the welcome of God's grace!

Experiencing life in community with diverse perspectives, people, and backgrounds can benefit us tremendously. There is reason to hope as we watch God meet people where they are at with his mercy. There are so many ways to express thanks, to live with authentic joy, and to show our uniqueness. Let's celebrate our differences, even as we are unified by love.

Don't be afraid to be different. Own your unique interests, passions, and gifts, and live authentically while loving your neighbor as yourself.

Preparation Is Key

The Lord All-Powerful says, "I will send my messenger, who will prepare the way for me. Suddenly, the Lord you are looking for will come to his Temple; the messenger of the agreement, whom you want, will come."

MALACHI 3:1 NCV

We do not go from one day hoping to the next living in the fullness of that hope. There is a time of preparation, and then a walking out step by step to get there. The journey requires patience, and the end requires consistent effort. Galatians 6:9 encourages us to "not become tired of doing good. We will receive our harvest of eternal life at the right time if we do not give up."

Perseverance is important, but so is the act of preparation. In hope, we prepare ourselves by setting ourselves up for success and longevity. We do this by being active members in supportive communities, by using tools for encouragement when we need it, and by sharing our hope with a trusted person in our lives. Don't worry, no matter where you are in your journey of hope, there is time to equip yourself here and now.

Share your hope with someone you trust. Sometimes simply sharing it can help you to move ahead.

Brilliant Light

A fountain of life was in him, for his life is light for all humanity. And this Light never fails to shine through darkness—Light that darkness could not overcome!

JOHN 1:4-5 TPT

The life of Christ is a bright light for all. The fountain of life, the source of all that we long for, is found in him. He can handle the fullness of our hope, because in him all hopes are fulfilled. Jesus Christ, who was, who is, and who is to come, is the center of our faith. He is the living expression of God; he made the unknowable knowable and the invisible visible.

As we give our hopes to him, we find that there is enough room for even more than we could imagine. Let's dare to dream big in his presence, and to expand our understanding in the great depths of his wisdom. He is so much better than the best of men!

Hope is an energetic force that helps us in so many regards. As you dream, hope, and put it into action, you move toward the brilliant light of God, ever closer to the source of all that you long for.

Long-awaited Answers

The angel said to him, "Do not be afraid, Zechariah, for your prayer has been heard, and your wife Elizabeth will bear you a son, and you shall call his name John.

LUKE 1:13 ESV

Zechariah and Elizabeth had waited a long time for a child. Miraculously in their old age they had a son, whom we know as John the Baptist. Naturally, it did not make sense for them to hope for a child, but God provided a miracle! Sometimes we may wait so long for an answer that we don't believe it's possible anymore. And sometimes God surprises us with a miraculous gift.

Abraham and Sarah experienced a similar situation. Romans 4:18 describes Abraham's belief this way, "In hope he believed against hope, that he should become the father of many nations, as he had been told." Sometimes the promises of God, and even our deep-seated desires, require us to hold on and hope.

There are some hopes that the timing is completely out of your hands. You can only keep believing and carry on until their answer finally comes. Surrender your hope to the Lord and keep hoping!

Glorify the Lord

"My soul magnifies the Lord, and my spirit rejoices in God my Savior, because he has looked with favor on the humble condition of his servant. Surely, from now on all generations will call me blessed."

LUKE 1:46-48 CSB

Mary was overwhelmed by the favor of God and by the honor she had to carry the Messiah. She didn't even know to desire such a thing. Sometimes, life's greatest surprises turn into our greatest blessings.

When we feel what Mary did, humble awe and reverence, let's do as she did: magnify the Lord and rejoice in him. When we feel blessed, let's offer that joy right back to the Lord! He is the giver of every good and perfect gift, and every time we thank him, we turn our hearts with intention toward him. He is so very worthy of our praise, and he is so very trustworthy with our hope!

Let every bit of joy, beauty, gratitude, and hope turn you to the Lord today. Thank him for his wonderful love and for his thoughtfulness toward you!

Count the Cost

"Don't begin until you count the cost. For who would begin construction of a building without first calculating the cost to see if there is enough money to finish it?"

LUKE 14:28 NLT

It is foolish to undertake a grand endeavor without figuring the cost first. This principle applies to more than our finances. We must consider the time, energy, and sacrifice it will take to accomplish our goal. Then we must weigh if it's worth it or not.

Wisdom applies to our hope as much as it does to the implementation of our practices and plans. If we have a hope to build a business, for instance, but we don't consider what owning and running a business will look like, we don't count the cost of the end, let alone what it will take to get there. As we weight the cost with the benefit, only we can decide whether it is worth it, though we can certainly lean on the advice and wisdom of others who have taken the same path.

With any hope, you should consider why we want it. If the purpose is only self-serving, it probably won't be enough to sacrifice for. On the other hand, if you count the cost and still think it worth it, then at least you know what you are getting into and what it will require.

Prayer and Praise

Is anyone among you suffering? Then he must pray.
Is anyone cheerful? He is to sing praises.

JAMES 5:13 NASB

Prayer is a powerful practice to help us unburden, open ourselves to different perspectives, and connect to something greater than us. Praise is an expression of joy that we offer to the giver of good gifts, the creator of the universe, and our savior. No matter where we find ourselves today, we can turn it either into prayer or praise.

Hope is built through connection, and this is true of our relationship with God. As we offer our prayers to him, we join our hearts to his faithfulness, letting go of the need to manage what we cannot control. Praise turns our celebration into an offering of gracious thanks to the God who is with us through it all. As we turn our hearts to the Lord in every circumstance, we cultivate deeper connection with the faithful one. As we see him come through for us, our praise fuels our hope, as well.

Pray about everything that weighs on your mind and offer to pray for those who are worried around you. There is power to fuel your hope and deepen your connection with Christ as you.

Blessing of Foresight

A good person leaves an inheritance
for their children's children,
but a sinner's wealth
is stored up for the righteous.

PROVERBS 13:22 NIV

If all our hopes begin and end with us, then we should venture
to dream bigger. Our lives are not lived in a vacuum. What we
do affects others, both for good and for harm. Foresight and
generational planning can be used as a blessing. Though we
cannot predict how things will play out to a tee, we can do our
best to plan for success with wisdom.

As we adjust our perspective to include how our actions will
ripple into the next generation (and the one after that), we are
able to choose what is beneficial not only to us in the present
moment, but what will benefit those who come after us. Hope
for our children should not remain simply in the realm of well
wishes. We can work to help them achieve the hopes we have
for them by sowing into their futures and setting them up well.
Our actions can and do connect to theirs.

*What hopes do you have for the following generation? Pick
one and sow into it in practical ways.*

Skilled Artisans

He has filled him with the Spirit of God, in wisdom
and understanding, in knowledge and all manner of
workmanship, to design artistic works, to work in gold and
silver and bronze.

EXODUS 35:31-32 NKJV

The arts are as important as technical jobs. There are many
forms of skilled work that reflect the wisdom of God through
the work of our hands. Whatever we do, whatever we put our
energy toward, if we submit to the Lord, his Spirit will move
through our efforts. Creative pursuits can be so incredibly
meaningful to us, and to the world around us. Let's not neglect
our creative hobbies.

We don't have to turn our hobbies into careers. They can
remain creative pursuits that fuel our souls. At the same time,
for those who are artists, musicians, and artisans by trade, we
should respect their craft as much as we do any other career.
Their art can inspire us in every area of life; what hope we
have as the Spirit moves in us as a response to what they have
created!

*Take time to look at some art, read poetry, or visit a building
built with beauty and form in mind. Ask the Spirit to meet and
inspire you as you do.*

True Life

Tell the rich people to do good, to be rich in doing good deeds, to be generous and ready to share. By doing that, they will be saving a treasure for themselves as a strong foundation for the future. Then they will be able to have the life that is true life.

1 TIMOTHY 6:18-19 NCV

Though many of us in the West would not consider ourselves rich by the standards we see in our culture, if we have more than enough food for today, a place to call home, and any bit of luxury, we have more than many in this world. Let's not neglect the encouragement of today's verse but apply it to our own lives.

Do good, be rich in doing good deeds, be generous, and ready to share. That is good advice for us all. Love reaches out. Generosity can be practiced, no matter how much we have in the bank (remember the widow's mite in Mark 12:42). True life is found as we let go of stuff and embrace our connection with others.

Sitting with what generosity would look like for you today, be intentional about reaching out, doing good, and not putting a limit on your kindness.

Making Room

"Give generously and generous gifts will be given back to you, shaken down to make room for more. Abundant gifts will pour out upon you with such an overflowing measure that it will run over the top! The measurement of your generosity becomes the measurement of your return."

Luke 6:38 tpt

The more generous we are, the more room we make to receive from God. When we hold too tightly to what we have, we may not realize that we are limiting what we can accept. Though God's kingdom is limitless, we are limited in our capacity. Think of a home: if you constantly store up things, you forget what you have. You run out of places to put them. There is no joy in hoarding, only self-protection. However, there is so much joy in generosity. The more we give, the more room we make.

In the expanse of generosity, we set the tone. In the scarcity of holding on tightly to what we have, we also set the tone. If we want to experience the generosity of God fully, we must participate in it!

Make room in your actual home, giving away what you no longer need (even if only a couple things) as a physical way to practice to this principle.

Reap What You Sow

Whoever sows sparingly will also reap sparingly, and whoever sows bountifully will also reap bountifully. Each one must give as he has decided in his heart, not reluctantly or under compulsion, for God loves a cheerful giver.

2 CORINTHIANS 9:6-7 ESV

A key component of hope is actively engaging in activities or steps that lead you to it. If you don't sow anything into it, it remains simply a wish. There's nothing wrong with wishing, but it is important to recognize that hope requires our action, not just our belief.

When it comes to our finances, jobs, relationships—you name it—we get much more out of them when we intentionally invest in them. Anything else is simply chance. It's time to take ownership in the dreams we have by working toward them, all while implementing the values of God's kingdom that we are mandated to follow. It may sound like a lot, but it's not. It's our work to do! God can handle all the things we cannot, and not only that, but we also have his help every step of the way.

Choose a hope to sow into this month, and work toward it step by step with consistent action.

Walk in the Light

If we walk in the light as he himself is in the light, we have fellowship with one another, and the blood of Jesus his Son cleanses us from all sin.

1 JOHN 1:7 CSB

When we walk in the ways of God, we walk in the light of his presence. It's important that we adopt his ways as our own, promoting justice, integrity, and kindness with our lifestyles. The ways of this world are full of shadows of shame, greed, and control. These can show up in church systems, as well. With wisdom, we know to test the fruit and not only take people at their word if we truly want to trust them. Evidence is in the fruit.

The fruit of the Spirit are laid out for us in Galatians 6. The things we should set our minds upon are listed in Philippians 4:8. Too many religious leaders exemplify judgment and hate, and that is not of God. The things that unify us in fellowship—mercy, justice, and peace—are filled with the light of Christ. Let's be sure we are living with God's values as our own.

The truth of Christ is important, and it is imperative that you test your heart considering it. He cleanses you from sin, and you walk in his ways. As you do, you are drenched in the light of his grace.

Goodness of God

You are not like that, for you are a chosen people. You are royal priests, a holy nation, God's very own possession. As a result, you can show others the goodness of God, for he called you out of the darkness into his wonderful light.

1 PETER 2:9 NLT

Isaiah 61 describes the power of God's love through the ministry of his people. The redeemed get to share the goodness of God with those who have yet to experience it.

If we have any hope in Christ, any hunger in him, it will be satisfied in his love. We don't have to fear the trials that come or the pain we cannot escape because the presence of God with us is our strength. Every step we take, he is there. Every time we call out for him, he answers with a Father's help! What goodness is in store for all who wait on the Lord!

Hope speaks possibility into dire situations. Have you experienced the goodness of God in your struggles? If so, share that with someone today.

Better Together

Two are better than one because they have a good return
for their labor; for if either of them falls, the one will lift up
his companion. But woe to the one who falls when there is
not another to lift him up!

ECCLESIASTES 4:9-10 NASB

Not only do our relationships benefit from hope, but hope
is also strengthened in relationship. With shared goals,
patience, and trust, we can work toward the hope we have
together. This way, if one of us falls, the other can lift us up.
Encouragement is a powerful tool to keep us moving in the
direction we want to go.

Not every hope is a shared one, but those that are can be
made stronger as we join in partnership with another. As
we meet to keep up the momentum, divide the work, and
problem solve challenges, we benefit from the strength,
creativity, and support that multiple people bring to the
table. If we are struggling in hope, perhaps we need the right
connections. It can make all the difference!

*Partnerships can be incredibly powerful, especially with a
unified vision and the commitment to seeing it through. Is
there a hope you have that would benefit from partnership?
Explore what that would look like.*

In It All

One God and Father of all,
who is over all and through all and in all.

EPHESIANS 4:6 NIV

God is the perfect Father. He does not work in some of his children and not in others. To all who come to him, he offers the abundance of his being. He is always full of mercy, patience, and peace. He is just, kind, and powerful. It is this God who remains over all, through all, and in all.

If our hope lies solely in what we can offer, it is too small. Hope is something to work toward that remains beyond our reach in the moment. We can take steps, but God can do far more. As we offer him ourselves, we trust him with the things we can't account for. He is better than we can ever imagine, so let's not stop putting our trust in him along the way, even as we offer what we can. There is so much grace to meet us in every moment. His presence is near; in him we find what we are looking for, so we must not neglect pursuing him. He is easy to find and easy to please!

See if you can spot the nature of God in the people, places, and nature around you. Every time you spot an attribute in the wild, remind yourself that this reflects the God who works in you.

Lifegiving Faith

"For God so loved the world that He gave His only begotten Son, that whoever believes in Him should not perish but have everlasting life."

JOHN 3:16 NKJV

God did not just tell us that he loves us. He showed it with flesh and bones. He revealed it in Christ. In the same way, if we say that we hope for something but don't live it out, it is an empty hope. James 2 says that faith without works is as good as dead. In verse 18 James says, "But someone will say, 'You have faith, and I have works.' Show me your faith without your works, and I will show you my faith by my works." In short, we live out what we truly believe.

The same is true with our hope. If we have hope for breakthrough, then we take steps toward it. If we have a goal that we want to reach in life, we must put in the work to do our part to get there. Lifegiving faith is found in Christ, and that faith is revealed by how we live!

Belief and desire pair together to move you in hope. What is a belief that you have that you are not reflecting in your lifestyle? What are you going to do to change that?

Propagate Hope

We ask you, brothers and sisters,
to warn those who do not work.
Encourage the people who are afraid.
Help those who are weak.
Be patient with everyone.

1 THESSALONIANS 5:14 NCV

Encouragement can help those who are afraid to persevere. Helping those who are weak lifts the burden of having to go it alone. Being patient with others shows understanding and encourages atmospheres of compassion. These are all important ways to build hope in people. If we want to see our communities transformed by the power of hope, then creating atmospheres where it can grow is paramount.

Hope is an important resource for coping in hard times, strengthening mindsets and resolve, and it dynamically motivates us to keep moving head. Every aspect of hope is best served in community. If we find that the people around us are hopeless, we can look for practical ways we can offer support, presence, and tools. There is limitless potential for positive impact when we put hope into action in our communities!

Pick a part of today's verse to put into practice in your community.

Think On It

Mary treasured all these things in her heart
and often pondered what they meant.

LUKE 2:19 TPT

There are some things so close to our heart that we need to ponder them in our hearts and minds before we bring them to anyone else. We may spend years quietly treasuring the beauty of what the Lord has spoken to us, and there is nothing wrong with that. Mary's act of treasuring the words that the angel had spoken to her was a private and meaningful one. It's okay for us to nurture the vulnerable things and keep them close.

One way to actively treasure what God sparks in us is to journal it. That way, we can keep it close and in a place that we can return to. We can read through how that shifts and transforms in time, as well as get our thoughts out on paper. Journaling has been shown to increase our feelings of peace and happiness, calming stress hormones in the process. Processing what is important to us, our reactions to it, and other life events can happen as well on paper as it can in conversation, so don't overlook this powerful tool.

Take time to write out the things that you have been coming back to in your heart and thoughts.

Signs from God

The Lord himself will give you a sign.
Behold, the virgin shall conceive and bear a son,
and shall call his name Immanuel.

ISAIAH 7:14 ESV

God knows us in our humanity. He knows that we need reassurance, and we need direction. He offers this in many ways. Prophets foretold the Messiah's coming long before Jesus was born in Bethlehem. God revealed the way he would be born, and these were signs that the Messiah had come.

When we want to decipher whether God is present in the promise, it is important that we look at the details surrounding it. Is there a sign that he has given to point to it? Does it make sense for us to go toward? Does his Spirit lead us that way? Not every hope requires a sign, but if you find yourself in need of direction, ask the Lord to help you. He is a faithful leader. He will not leave you, even if you start down your own path. He will bring direction and redirection as necessary!

It is important to lay claim to your hope through your own steps, and it is also important to reevaluate the end if you decide to go a different way. The Lord in his faithfulness will always follow through; that's not your work to do. Lean on his help, trust him, and keep your eyes open.

Overwhelmed by Hope

When they saw the star,
they were overwhelmed with joy.

MATTHEW 2:10 CSB

When the wise men saw the star in the sky over a house in Bethlehem, they were overjoyed. Their journey had taken them several days, probably about twelve, to arrive from the desert where they had originated. They had known the star was a sign of the Messiah, and they followed it in faith.

Having reached their destination, their joy was full! This is what it is like to reach the pinnacle of our hope. We set out on the journey, walking toward it in faith, and we do what we can to get there. There may be challenges along the way, but when we reach it, oh the joy that we feel! It is always worth it to follow the pull of our hearts in faith as it takes us to places, we can only dream of.

Recall a time that you were filled with the satisfaction of joy after a long journey (this can be a metaphorical one). Was it worth all the trouble to get there? Thank God for that taste of fulfilled hope and remember it when you need a reminder to keep pressing on in other areas.

God With Us

"Look! The virgin will conceive a child!
She will give birth to a son,
and they will call him Immanuel,
which means 'God is with us.'"

MATTHEW 1:23 NLT

The power of Immanuel, God with us, is as palpable today as it was when Jesus walked the earth. Not only did God send his Son, but he also sent us his Spirit. With the Spirit's fellowship, we have access to the fullness of God: his love, joy, peace, patience, kindness, gentleness, and power. We have the presence of God *with us* even now!

Everything we need originates in God. He owns the cattle on a thousand hills, as Psalm 50 states. He has all the resources to nourish us, to keep us safe, and to empower us in his kingdom ways. Jesus revealed that God's heart has always been to dwell with his people. The tabernacle, the holy of holies, was not close enough. The Father sent Jesus to tear the veil and bring himself to the people, and the people the freedom to come to him!

What impact does "God with us" have on you? Reflect on what the power of God's presence with you means for your hope, your life, and your dreams.

Prince of Peace

A Child will be born to us, a Son will be given to us;
And the government will rest on His shoulders;
And His name will be called Wonderful Counselor,
Mighty God, Eternal Father, Prince of Peace.

ISAIAH 9:6 NASB

Jesus Christ came to set the sinner free, to heal the sick, and to bring resurrection life and hope to all who believe in him. He did not come to condemn the world, but to save it. He is the Prince of Peace. This remains true today.

How does our faith align with this truth? Do we error on the side of condemnation and judgment, or do we extend and pursue peace because Christ is the king of peace? There is so much hope in him; he is Wonderful Counselor, Mighty God, and the living expression of the Eternal Father! In him, we see the heart of God on display. We cannot ignore Christ's teachings, his ministry, or his lifestyle if we want to reflect him in our own lives. We get to join his heart by proclaiming the Lord's favor revealed through his love (Luke 4:19).

Promote peace and lay down your weapons (thoughtless words) while you spend time with those you love today.

Carry On in Hope

This is the testimony:
God has given us eternal life,
and this life is in his Son.

1 JOHN 5:11 NIV

Every day we journey in this life, if we remember Christ with us, there is a hope that will not fail. When our bodies reach their natural end, there lies something more on the other side of death: eternal life. That is our ultimate hope in this life, and it will not disappoint!

When we root our lives in Christ, he is the soil, the water, and the nutrients that feed us. He is our source of living water. If we want life, we do well to bind our hearts to Christ and to follow him on his path of laid-down love. There is no better way. Even when there are droughts and storms, his presence faithfully remains. We never need to venture even a moment in this life alone, so let's continue to carry on in hope!

How have you built your life on Christ? If you don't have an answer, yield your heart to him today and allow him to lead you in his love. It is as practical as it is powerful!

Know Your Reason

Being found in appearance as a man, He humbled Himself and became obedient to the point of death, even the death of the cross. Therefore God also has highly exalted Him and given Him the name which is above every name.

PHILIPPIANS 2:8-9 NKJV

We can learn so much from the life of Jesus. Though we don't know much about most of his life or how that played out, even that is a beautiful picture for us. In the normalcy and the growing, the changes and transitions, God is working in us. When Jesus began his ministry, he knew the purpose underlying it. He could endure all the challenges, even death on a cross, because he knew the power of its purpose and what lay ahead of him.

If we don't have meaning behind our hope, even if it's a deeply personal one, we will give up when challenges arise. However, if we are convinced of our purpose, we can keep persevering through the hard times with that hope and motivation intact. It's so important to know our reason!

What is the driving force of the hopes you have? Is there a deeper meaning, or a conviction for what you are working toward? It doesn't have to be as big as Jesus' was (it all pales in comparison!), but you must know the reason, nonetheless.

Just Do Your Best

Whatever work you do, do your best, because you are going to the grave, where there is no working, no planning, no knowledge, and no wisdom.

ECCLESIASTES 9:10 NCV

Hope helps us to face challenges with resilience. It invites us to grow as we take on goals that are bigger than ourselves. Hope doesn't pacify us in our comfort zones; it pulls us out of them and reorients our mindsets. We will not become superhuman by harnessing hope, but we can certainly do our best and let go of the rest

Hard work is exemplified in Scripture. Proverbs 14:23 says, "those who work hard make a profit, but those who only talk will be poor." Certainly, our salvation is a gift of grace. There is no question in that; we can't strive to become right with God. We receive the invitation of Christ's freedom as we come to him! Knowing this, we cannot overlook the importance of doing our best in every area, though. Our confidence in Christ should cause us to be more willing to do the work that is ours to do with gratitude and dedication!

Is there something that you have been talking about doing but have not made any headway in? Figure your next steps and take them.

Cling to Him

No matter what, I will continue to hope and passionately cling to Christ, so that he will be openly revealed through me before everyone's eyes. So I will not be ashamed! In my life or in my death, Christ will be magnified in me.

PHILIPPIANS 1:20 TPT

When we prioritize our relationship with Christ, everything else will flow from that. Jesus put it this way: "above all, constantly seek God's kingdom and his righteousness, then all these less important things will be given to you abundantly" (Matthew 6:33). As we cling to Jesus and seek his kingdom first, we can rest assured that we will have all we need.

Looking to Christ as our day begins, as we go through it, and at the end of it can keep our focus on his perspective through it all. We can invite in his wisdom, even as we do our best to align our choices with his love. He is a faithful friend, and he is always there when we need him.

Keep an open line of prayer from sunup to sundown and turn your attention to Christ as often as you think of it today.

Open Door

"I am the way, and the truth, and the life.
No one comes to the Father except through me."

JOHN 14:6 ESV

Of all the hopes we have in this life, there is none more worthwhile of a pursuit than God himself. Jesus opened the way to the Father, ushering us into his presence. We don't have to wait for a priest to go to him on our behalf. Wherever we are, no matter the time or circumstance, we can go to the throne of grace with confidence because of Christ.

Jesus said that he is the way, the truth, and the life. If we are looking for a way to go, we cannot go wrong by going to him first. If we are searching for the truth, we will find it in the person of Jesus. If we are looking for the meaning of life, and for the joy of life, we will find it as we come alive in his presence. He is our open door to the Father and to the great expanse of his kingdom. Let's go to him first and go to him often!

If you need a refresh for your hope, your joy, your peace, and so much more, you can find it in the fellowship of Christ. Prioritize time with the Lord this week and see what difference it makes to your life!

Fresh and New

Put on the new self, the one created according to God's
likeness in righteousness and purity of the truth.

EPHESIANS 4:24 CSB

As we live in union with Christ, fellowshipping with his Spirit
and transforming in his limitless love, we practice putting
on the new self that he has created for us. We don't die to
our personality or our preferences, but the chains of our
fear, shame, and fruitless cycles certainly are broken. Being
fresh and new in Christ is like being born again, with all the
goodness of who we are lit from the inside and free from the
junk that weighed us down.

Knowing that there is a new start available and goodness
beyond what we have even yet known, hope propels us
forward. It is more than excitement; it is belief, anticipation,
desire, and all that they incorporate. What would the relief of
a fresh start mean to you today? Perhaps that is right where
Christ wants to restore you in hope.

*Take time to dream big about the coming year (and beyond!)
with God. Just get it all out there. You can go back through
your list and decide the areas you want to really focus in on
and harness practical hope in the coming week.*